Overhead Cost

Overhead Cost

JOHN INNES
The University of Dundee

and

FALCONER MITCHELL
The University of Edinburgh

|C| I |*m*| A |

Published in association with
The Chartered Institute of Management Accountants

ACADEMIC PRESS
Harcourt Brace & Company, Publishers
London San Diego New York
Boston Sydney Tokyo Toronto

ACADEMIC PRESS LTD.
24/28 Oval Road,
London NW1 7DX

United States Edition published by
ACADEMIC PRESS INC.
San Diego, California 92101–4311

A catalogue record for this book is available from the British Library

ISBN 0–12 372140–7

Typeset by Photo·graphics, Honiton, Devon
Printed and bound in Great Britain by Mackays of Chatham plc,
Chatham, Kent

Series Editor's Preface

David Ottley
KPMG Peat Marwick Professor of Accounting
Lancaster University

A major problem for the management accounting teacher has been the selection of a suitable text for advanced courses. Although a number of very good texts exist, they typically do not include some topics that individual teachers wish to teach. On the other hand, they do include a considerable amount of material on topics that are unnecessary for a particular course. Students often feel that they have a poor deal in purchasing large and expensive texts that do not cover the whole of their course, yet include large amounts of extraneous material.

This series is an attempt to resolve this problem. It will consist of a set of slim volumes, each of which deals with a single topic in depth. A coherent course of study may therefore be built up by selecting just those topics which an individual course requires, so that the student has a tailor-made text for the precise course that is being taken. The texts are aimed primarily at final year undergraduate courses in accounting and finance, although many will be suitable for MBA and other postgraduate programmes. A typical final year advanced management accounting option course could be built around four or five texts, as each has been designed to incorporate material that would be taught over a period of a few weeks. Alternatively, the texts can be used to supplement a larger and more general textbook.

Each text is a free-standing treatment of a specific topic by an authoritative author. They can be used quite independently of each other, although it is assumed that an introductory or intermediate-level management accounting course has been previously taken. However, considerable care has been taken in the choice and specification of topics, to ensure that the texts mesh together without unnecessary overlap. It is therefore hoped that the series will provide a valuable resource for management accounting teachers, enabling them to design courses that meet precise needs whilst still being able to recommend required texts at an affordable price.

Acknowledgements

The authors would like to acknowledge The Chartered Institute of Management Accountants and the Canon Foundation in Europe (both authors have held Canon Fellowships) for, over a number of years, funding research which has been drawn on heavily in writing this text. Our gratitude is also due to Caroline Hall who expertly handled the manuscript typing, to an anonymous CIMA reviewer for useful comments and to David Otley for his valuable editorial advice on our initial manuscript draft.

Contents

1

The Nature of Overhead Costs

INTRODUCTION

Overhead costs have long provided a series of challenges and problems for accountants and managers. Indeed some of the earliest publications on the subject of management accounting focus on the practical difficulties of overhead costing (e.g. Solomons, 1968; Parker, 1969). Much of this early work has stood the test of time well, and several current practices in the area are, in fact, closely akin to those which were originally developed around a century ago.

However, some developments have also been evident since then, with particular attention being devoted to this class of cost, by both practitioners and academics, during the last decade. The result is an area of cost accounting with an extensive literature and with a current topicality engendered by the recent advocacy of activity-based costing as one means of addressing some of the difficulties which overhead costing and management can pose.

As a topic, overhead cost exposes and highlights many of the limitations of the discipline of accounting, but, as this text will show, it also demonstrates the accountant's resilience and ingenuity in "delivering" at the "sharp end" of the information business. To provide a foundation for examining accounting approaches to measuring, analysing and managing overhead cost, this chapter

1

Table 1.1 Accounting cost classifications.

Input ─────────▶ Process ─────────▶ Output		
Type of resource acquired	*Application or use of resource*	*End results of resource acquisition and use*
● Materials and supplies ● Labour ● Bought-in services	● Production support ● Production ● Administration ● Distribution ● Marketing	● Range of final products/services (segmented in various ways e.g. – type of product – location – status – sold/unsold

explores the meaning of cost and the nature and significance of overhead as one important element of it.

COSTS

The *Official Terminology* of the Chartered Institute of Management Accountants (1991) defines cost in the following terms:

(as a noun) The amount of expenditure (actual or notional) incurred on, or attributable to, a specified thing or activity.

(as a verb) To ascertain the cost of a specified thing or activity.

The word cost can rarely stand alone and should be qualified as to its nature and limitations.

Applying this definition involves ascertaining the acquisition price of an item or service which has been purchased and using that information as a basis for costing either the resource acquired (e.g. raw material, electric power) or the use or end purpose to which it has been put (e.g. the process of assembling parts or the particular final product or service output achieved). The focus of cost is typically known as the cost object.

However, other views and measures of cost are also available. For example, the replacement cost of a resource could be ascertained by estimating its current rather than historic acquisition cost, and this may well provide a more realistic indication of the forthcoming sacrifice which will be necessary if resource consumption is to be followed by replacement. Also, the economist views cost in terms of the best opportunities forgone by choosing to apply resources to particular ends. This perspective is especially pertinent to the taking of decisions on how best to use resources. However, measurements of these notions of cost are not usually routinely available – they normally require specific estimations and judgements to be made in the context of a particular situation at a particular time.

In contrast, acquisition cost information is readily available from conventional double-entry based accounting systems and is backed by the documentary evidence of specific transactions. Thus the accountant's routine approach to costing is based on historic acquisition costs. As the above definition suggests, they bear descriptive qualifications which, in conventional accounting systems, are usually related either to the type of input which they represent or the process to which they are applied or the final process output which is achieved. Table 1.1 outlines these typical classifications.

3

COST ELEMENTS

The nature of overhead costs can also be explained by reference to the framework provided in Table 1.1. Any organization will acquire the three basic types of resource in the input cell. The resources acquired will be applied to various purposes which ultimately contribute to the organization's end results. While the accountant will be involved in tracking their application, they are normally initially classified in the manner set out below. This four-way categorization both reflects the type of resource acquired and the degree of association which it has with final product or service outputs.

1. *Direct material* The physical components of an output which can be directly associated with it. It is all represented by material content – for example, the wood in a table which can be physically identified and measured. It can also be traced to the transaction(s) involved in its acquisition and the price paid used as a basis for its cost.
2. *Direct labour* The productive work undertaken by employees to convert direct materials into finished output. It is all represented by employees' labour. Again the resource can be directly linked to output through the monitoring and recording of time spent working on a particular product. The wages payment transaction provides the basic cost data which time sheets allow to be directly associated with individual products.
3. *Direct expenses* These represent other resources (usually services) acquired which can be clearly and directly associated with specific outputs; for example, where a royalty payment is made for the use of a patented idea in the production of a certain product, or where power used in a particular product is metered and accurate records are kept to show its application to product lines.
4. *Overheads (or indirect costs)* All of the residual resources acquired are termed overheads. They range in type from supplies (e.g. oil, stationery) to labour (supervision) to services (light and heat). They also contribute to the various processes undertaken within an organization, but one overhead (e.g. general management, rent of buildings) may often relate to several processes. Moreover, they have in common the characteristic that they are not or cannot be directly associated, through the costing system, with particular product or service outputs.

4

THE OVERHEAD COST ELEMENT

Overhead costs are therefore diverse in terms of the types of inputs which they represent. As outlined above, they are normally defined by reference to the product or service output of the organization concerned and differentiated from direct costs by the low degree of association which they have with this cost object. Although overheads are usually defined in this way, the notion of overhead costs can also be applied in respect of other cost objects. Thus overhead in relation to the divisions within an organization could include centrally incurred administration costs, while in relation to geographical market segments they might include national promotion and advertising expenses. However, the term is more commonly used in relating costs to product or service output, and in this text it is primarily used in this way.

While variety is one of the salient characteristics of overhead, it is possible to describe their composition in terms of three broad categories of input cost:

1. Costs which cannot be definitively associated with the product because their incurrence is common to a variety of outputs; for example, the occupancy costs or general management of a production facility.
2. Costs which could be directly associated with products but which, on grounds of materiality and/or convenience, are not. For example, a furniture manufacturer will often treat the cost of nails and glue as an overhead, rather than suffering the trouble and expense of establishing a system of recording the usage of these resources for each unit of output as a basis for establishing cost.
3. Costs which are directly associated with individual products but which are deemed to be more appropriately treated as relating to all output. For example, the overtime premium paid to production employees will be linked to specific output through the time sheet records which are maintained. However, the creation of the need for overtime working may be viewed as the result of general product demand exceeding capacity. The selection of particular output to be produced in overtime may be merely one of chance, depending on the timing of the order and the production schedule. Thus the extra cost of the overtime is a cost which should be treated as attributable to all output, not simply to the units directly associated with it.

Table 1.2 Overhead – typical examples.

Categorized by type of input	*Categorized by type of process*
1. Labour not directly attributable to production work, e.g. operational supervision, technical service provision, management.	1. Production processes and resources which support production. This comprises the overhead which can be specifically related to either the general area of production or to particular processes within it although it cannot be attributed directly to products, e.g. machine insurance and depreciation.
2. Supplies and materials purchased to assist in the general running of the organization, e.g. lubricants and spare parts for machinery, stationery, overalls and protective clothing.	2. Production service processes, e.g. maintenance, scheduling, set-up and change, quality control, material storage and handling.
3. Services purchased to support the general running of the organization, e.g. insurance, power, rates, rent, printing, telephone, etc.	3. Administrative/managerial processes, e.g. customer order processing, purchasing, accounting, planning, personnel.
4. Depreciation which represents the cost of services provided by capital assets such as buildings, machines and equipment.	4. Sales, distribution and marketing processes, e.g. salesmen visits, product delivery, promotion and advertising.

These three categories include costs representing a range of inputs which are attributable to a number of process activities. The detailed composition of overhead costs will vary as the existence of many overhead costs in any particular organization is dependent on the nature of that organization and the materiality of the individual costs. The latter issue will be influential in determining whether a system will be established to treat the cost as a direct expense, or whether it will simply constitute a category 2 type of overhead.

Table 1.2 contains a listing of typical types of overhead designated both at the input and use/application stages. These are simply two alternative ways of analysing the same total overhead cost. They indicate respectively what resource has been acquired (input) and how it has been used (process). The two views of overhead contained in Table 1.2 illustrate and describe the main components of this class of cost. In a costing system the initial capture of information will be from the transactions which underlie their acquisition. These will reflect the nature of the inputs to the process. Thus the payment of wages or salaries, the recognition of depreciation from an acquired capital asset and the accrual of power or insurance on the receipt of their respective bills will initiate recognition of the cost and provide a basis for its segmentation in the ledger records to reflect the type of input acquired. The input analysis primarily shows what resources have been acquired. It is then a matter of costing system design as to how these costs are further analysed and reported. However they are seldom simply left in their input categories, and normally at least a partial classification in terms of their application within processes will be attempted. Thus the process analysis will show how the acquired resources have been utilized within the organization. In addition, the costing system will usually provide information on the unitization of overhead. This involves sharing it out to the individual units of the final output of the process; the procedures and issues which this involves form the basis of Chapter 2.

THE VARIED DIMENSIONS OF OVERHEAD COST

As outlined above, overheads can be readily described in terms of either the inputs or the specific process applications of the resources which they represent within the organization. Additionally it is also possible to analyse them in alternative ways which provide further, useful insights into the nature and the manner in which they can be treated and reported by the costing system of an organization.

Production v. non-production overhead

This is an important distinction, not simply because of the perspective which it gives on the pattern of cost incurrence, but also because of the need to segregate these two types of cost for stock valuation. It is only production overhead which can be included in the unit product costs which are used to value stocks for external reporting purposes. There is some element of judgement in the split, although Statement of Standard Accounting Practice 9 (SSAP 9) specifies that stock value can include expenditure incurred "in bringing the product or service to its present location and condition".

This clearly incorporates all direct costs and overheads to the extent that they have been associated with the units before shipping them to the customer. Thus marketing and sales costs are clearly excluded, but within distribution and administration there will be many grey areas. The application of the prudence concept (which here would mitigate against the overstatement of the asset value and profitability) would tend to mitigate against the inclusion of any of these categories of cost, but a strict application even of the SSAP 9 definition could legitimize the inclusion in stock of:

- movement and distribution of stocks and raw materials within the organization;
- the procurement of supplies, parts and services;
- the administration of the production activity, e.g. throughput scheduling.

All other overheads which relate to the processes involved in selling output are not attributable to unsold goods and should therefore be excluded from the cost of stock. That is not to say, however, that these costs should not be incorporated in the unit cost information which is to be used for other purposes, e.g. pricing or decision-making.

Fixed v. variable overhead

To understand, explain and predict cost it is valuable to gain an appreciation of how it behaves. This knowledge provides a basis for the provision of cost information in decision-making and for the setting of budgets to aid cost control. Accountants have traditionally approached this task in a fairly narrow way. They have characterized cost behaviour in terms of a two-way split, costs being classed as either fixed or variable with respect to the volume of output. This split is normally made on the basis of the assumptions of a fairly short-term time perspective and a linear relationship between the two variables.

Conventionally the variable category includes direct material and direct labour, although the contemporary secure employment policies of some firms do cast some doubt on the categorization of the latter type of cost in this way. Also included is a portion of the overhead cost, e.g. machine lubrication, maintenance and power. Thus overhead cost has to be split into its fixed and variable categories. This requires the exercise of some judgement, especially if done purely by an *ad hoc* review of each overhead cost. A more accurate separation may be achieved by a statistical analysis, normally of past cost and volume data, along the lines of the alternatives shown in Example 1.1.

EXAMPLE 1.1

Separating fixed and variable overhead cost

Data:

Month	Total overhead cost (£)	Units of output
1	623 000	207 000
2	526 000	151 000
3	410 000	87 000
4	401 000	80 000
5	528 000	146 000
6	594 000	184 000
7	682 000	237 000
8	694 000	263 000
9	702 000	265 000
10	757 000	280 000
11	820 000	284 000
12	763 000	265 000
13	699 000	261 000
14	641 000	222 000
15	520 000	145 000

Separation of fixed and variable cost elements

1. High/low method

	Output (units)	Overhead cost (£)
Highest observation	284 000	820 000
Lowest observation	80 000	401 000
Difference	204 000	419 000

Thus the variable cost estimated from the difference in the two observations is £419 000 (i.e. the total cost variation) ÷ 204 000 (i.e. the total output variation) = £2.05. Using this estimate the fixed cost would be £237 000 computed at the low point as follows: [£401 000 − (80 000 × £2.05)].

2. Statistical regression★

The application of regression analysis to the above data produces a line of best fit described by the following equation:

Total overhead cost = 256 387 + 1.79 (output volume)

Thus the fixed cost estimate by this method is £256 387 and variable unit cost £1.79.

Discussion

Both of the above methods provide estimates of the fixed/variable overhead cost split. The first does this on the basis of only two of the fifteen observations and its result must therefore be regarded with some caution. Where, for example, economies of scale became highly influential at the high point, the estimate would be distorted. The statistical regression uses all of the available data but does assume that the relationship between overhead cost and output is linear. It therefore also only provides an approximation of the split. Many factors other than volume (e.g. technology changes and supplier price changes) will also influence overhead cost. It is therefore important to identify how much of the overhead cost variation is explained by output changes. The correlation coefficient allows this to be assessed. In the above example it is 0.984 and this indicates a strong association between

---

★For detailed explanation, see Kazmier, 1989; for more complex applications see Kaplan and Atkinson, 1989.

the two variables (a perfect linear correlation has a correlation coefficient of 1).

The results of this type of analysis are only as good as the extent and quality of data used. These attributes are often questionable due to the cost/output relationship being distorted by changes in organization, technology or by the impact of inflation. Another major limitation is the fact that some costs will be semi-variable (e.g. where discounts are received for volume acquisitions) and others step variable (e.g. where an extra machine is provided). The real pattern of overhead cost behaviour may therefore be more in line with that shown in Figure 1.1. The use of a linear surrogate for this may be reasonable over a small range of output variation, but clearly has the potential to mislead at certain volume levels and in estimating the impact of major changes in output volume on overhead costs.

One further area of distortion in the overhead cost/volume relationship is attributable to the fact that output characteristics other than volume will often influence cost. Changes in the

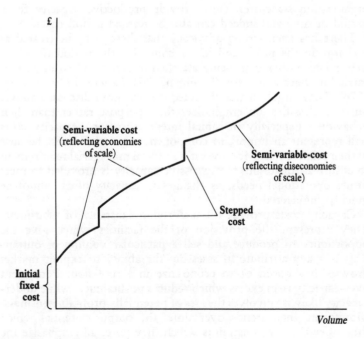

FIGURE 1.1 Overhead cost behaviour.

quality, variety and speed of delivery of the output and in the underlying flexibility and organization of production will also drive overhead. The modification of conventional cost behaviour analysis to take account of these factors is discussed in more detail in Chapter 4 on activity-based costing.

Capacity v. output costs

While all resources can be viewed as contributing to the capacity to operate in the short-run, in the longer term certain costs pertain to those resources which are associated with the provision of facilities which provide a more permanent core ability simply to operate, independent of any particular output level. As such they contrast with those costs which are dependent on a particular level of throughput achieved in the short term (direct material, piece-work labour). Into the former category would come the occupancy costs of a production facility (depreciation, rent), the costs associated with the existence of equipment (depreciation and insurance) and the supervisory and management costs of a chosen organization structure. They provide productive capacity for a period of time and indeed can also be termed period costs.

There has been strong advocacy that these costs be treated as a charge in the profit and loss account for the period to which they relate, rather than being attached to stock and so in part be carried forward as an asset (Fremgen, 1964; Largay, 1973; Swalley, 1974). They largely match the fixed cost category discussed above, but this classification emphasizes their purpose rather than their behaviour. Especially in capital intensive sectors, capacity costs will represent an important component of overhead cost because of their relative size. Moreover it is a crucial managerial requirement to ensure adequate but not excessive capacity is provided to meet future operational needs, as changes in capacity often cannot be quickly engineered.

Capacity costs provide the underlying substance of a business. They represent the provision of the facilities which give the opportunity to produce and sell a particular volume of output. This is a key attribute in assessing the ability to exploit market growth in a boom or to economize in a recession. Permanent over-capacity is an excess which reduces profitability, while under-capacity likewise involves the loss of potentially profitable business. Monitoring their trends over time, the output potential which they offer and the constraints which they pose, all emphasize the managerial significance of analysing this type of overhead.

Committed v. discretionary costs

Before a business begins, all costs can be termed discretionary, as the decisions which will lead to their being incurred will not yet have been taken. In the context of a going concern many costs, including a substantial overhead element, will have become committed, at least in the short run. For example, formal commitments will have been made through the signing of contracts which involve the rental of facilities or services. Furthermore, a less formal commitment is established for many costs through decisions made at the stage of planning the development of new projects and new products. In respect of the latter, Brimson (1986) emphasizes how pre-production management decisions constrain and determine the way in which products are made and the facilities and resources which will be employed in their manufacture (see Figure 1.2). These decisions commit the organization to a particular pattern of overhead cost. The selection of machinery involves a commitment to major elements of depreciation, insurance, maintenance and power. The layout and organization of production involves scheduling, supply and supervision costs. Changing these costs involves the time needed to re-equip and reorganize the business and to plan these developments effectively.

In contrast, other elements of overhead cost can be altered at management's discretion, in the short run. Indeed the susceptibility

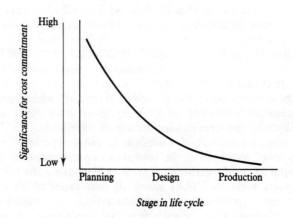

FIGURE 1.2 Cost commitment during the product life cycle.

13

of certain costs to reduction within a short time-scale has led to them being targeted as a convenient means of manipulating reported profits (Ferris, 1975; Griffiths, 1987). Thus training, advertising and repairs are all overheads which can be effectively changed in the short run. However, these are just the types of revenue expense which actually represent investment in the longer-run future. Their reduction may well lead to an immediate improvement in profit, but in the longer term, profitability may suffer.

FINANCIAL SIGNIFICANCE

The relative financial significance of overhead costs will vary from sector to sector, and indeed to some extent from business to business within a sector. Moreover, the nature of overhead will also vary in different situations. However, current trends towards increasing the range of product outputs, the customization of products, improvements in quality and in production scheduling as stocks are reduced, are all factors which increase the relative importance of overheads. Some evidence to support this rapid growth comes from the empirical analyses conducted by consultancy firms (Develin and Partners, 1990; IIR/Coopers & Lybrand Deloitte, 1989). They suggest that overheads have grown to average between one-third and one-half of total cost, and this is confirmed by other recent surveys (Innes and Mitchell, 1991a; Schwarsbach, 1985). More intensive competition, often international in nature, has also stimulated growth in sales and marketing related overheads: "5% of UK GNP is expended on direct marketing activities" (Piercy, 1986); "In many cases marketing expenditure accounts for up to 50% of the total costs of providing the goods or services" (Srikanthan *et al.*, 1987).

Finally, the summary of administration and distribution overheads disclosed in some recent UK company reports (see Table 1.3) shows two other categories of overhead which can clearly be important elements of cost in their own right and also contribute to the overall significance of overheads.

As administration and distribution costs represent only two sub-types of overhead in the companies concerned, they reinforce the importance of overhead, as well as illustrating the high degree of sectoral variation. Thus when all four types of overhead are considered (production, administration, distribution and sales/marketing) their relative financial significance is frequently considerable and in many instances is increasing, so providing

Table 1.3 Corporate non-production overhead.

	As % of total operating costs	
Company	Administration overhead %	Distribution overhead %
ICI (Chemicals)	23.7	7.9
Lonhro (conglomerate)	14.8	2.5
Whitbread (brewing)	14.1	2.2
Rothmans (tobacco)	10.3	3.4
Smiths Industries (electronics)	9.9	9.9
Taylor Woodrow (construction)	7.7	4.6
Unigate (food)	8.3	7.7
Burton (retail)	4.2	2.3

Source: Company Annual Reports, 1990–1.

fertile ground for the application of sound cost management practices.

OVERHEAD COST MANAGEMENT

As outlined above, overhead costs represent a substantial focus of cost incurrence and one which can be viewed from several perspectives. Each view which can be taken emphasizes particular attributes of this class of cost and so highlights another dimension which can assist in their measurement, analysis and management. For example, cost variability information is vital to decisions involving output volume changes, capacity cost information helps future planning, knowledge of cost commitments facilitates cost reduction exercises, costs of business processes allow benchmarking comparisons, and product costs enable stocks to be valued and profits measured. Moreover, only after their varied dimensions are understood and can be explained can their control be made effective. Thus information on each of the above views of overhead can prove valuable to managers.

Cost management is ultimately only as good as the information on which it is based, and management accountants have traditionally shown some neglect of the overhead cost area. Johnson and Kaplan (1987a) condemn the simple categorization of a large slice of overhead as fixed. In consequence, accountants tend to provide little supplementary information analysis on costs within this

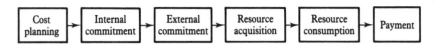

FIGURE 1.3 The process of cost incurrence.

classification. The realization that all costs can vary, but over different time-scales (Johnson and Kaplan, 1987b) emphasizes the poverty of this conventional accounting treatment. Fortunately, recent developments have addressed this area of difficulty (see Chapters 4, 5 and 6).

These ideas emphasize the fact that management of overhead cost should be based on an acknowledgement that incurred cost is not a discrete independent event but is the result of a process. As Figure 1.3 shows, cost incurrence is normally planned, internally authorized, externally committed, involves resource acquisition and consumption, and finally involves a payment.

In managing this process it is desirable to plan carefully with an accounting input at the earliest possible stage. This will ensure that commitments made will have taken account of relevant financial criteria. The acquisition of resources should be organized to occur as close to consumption as possible, so that payments are not made any earlier than is necessary. Finally it should be noted that consumption and payment are distinct stages in the process, with the amount of payments being derived ultimately from the amount of consumption.

The existence of a time lag here is also significant, as a reduction in consumption (e.g. in depreciation, in supplies, labour or services) may take time to work back to a reduction in spending (Cooper and Kaplan, 1991). As product cost information reflects resource consumption, it may not give a direct indication of how spending will be influenced, at least in the short run, by decisions affecting a particular product line. Thus an appreciation of cost incurrence as a process, not simply an event, is necessary to understand cost information and use it effectively in cost management.

DISCUSSION TOPICS

1. Identify the main cost objects which you consider relevant in a business context. Justify your choice.
2. The nature of overhead cost is multidimensional and the information generated to manage it must reflect this fact. Discuss.
3. The segmentation of costs into fixed and variable components is misleading, as management can take decisions which will change any cost. Do you agree?
4. What type of system would be required to enable the following costs to be treated as direct expenses rather than overheads?
   — maintenance;
   — canteen;
   — quality control inspection;
   — cleaning.
5. The key stage in the process of cost incurrence is that of internal commitment. Discuss with respect to accounting systems which recognize cost only at the stage of payment being made.

2

The Unitization of Overhead: the Traditional Approach

INTRODUCTION

Much of the early literature on overhead cost was concerned with the development of cost accounting techniques which would allow production overheads to be incorporated as one component of unit product costs (Solomons, 1968). The nature of overhead, described in the preceding chapter, indicates the cause of this preoccupation. Overheads, by definition, are not directly associated with individual products and the cost accountant has therefore been required to find an acceptable means of linkage to permit the generation of comprehensive product unit cost information for management. However if one is to attempt to assess the success of accountants in this work, it is necessary to appreciate not simply the technical aspects of the procedures and practices adopted, but also why unit costs are wanted in the first place. It is only by screening the cost accountant's output against the ultimate purpose to which it is put that its value can be properly assessed.

UNIT COST INFORMATION

Within organizations, unit cost information is required for a variety of reasons. These stem from the basic needs of management to plan, take decisions, measure and control operations and comply with legislation and professional requirements governing external reporting. The extent to which variation in these management needs requires to be satisfied by different unit cost information should be one of the major concerns of cost accounting. Therein also lies one of the current weaknesses of the discipline. For example, all too often the outputs of a system generating unit cost information which is designed primarily to satisfy the need for stock valuation are used without modification for other purposes by management (Kaplan, 1988). The utility of information must always be judged by reference to the purpose to which it is put. The most common purposes of unit cost information production are described below.

Stock valuation

Accounting convention requires that stocks be valued at the lower of cost or net realizable value. Only exceptionally will the latter valuation be used, as this would indicate an absence of profitability in the product concerned. Consequently the cost of units produced has to be computed in order to place a monetary value on this current asset. In the UK, for external reporting to shareholders, this value can include direct material, direct labour and all overheads incurred in getting the stock to its condition and location at the time of valuation. All production overheads are therefore normally included, and although no specific standard exists on the detail of how to do this, it has traditionally had to be done in a manner which can be considered "true and fair". This is achieved through the types of procedure and practice described in Example 2.2 below (pp. 32–35). The implications of costing stock are twofold:

1. An asset value is established.
2. The production costs not attaching to stock represent the cost of sales and this, in turn, determines the profit figure for the organization.

Assets are defined by accountants as items, owned by an organization, which will generate future economic benefits (positive cash flows) for it. This is a definition which holds some ambiguity, centring on the treatment of overheads, for costing purposes. Two interpretations are possible. On the one hand the future benefits of stock can be viewed in terms of the sales revenue which it will generate. Although this will exceed even a full production cost valuation, it is this cost which will normally be close to the output value. On the other hand the future economic benefit of holding stocks can be viewed in terms of the saving in future cost which is generated by its possession (Horngren and Sorter, 1962). This saving will comprise only variable costs as fixed costs, providing the capacity to produce for a period of time would not usually be affected by the existence of stocks. Thus variable cost gives an input perspective on the asset's benefit to the organization.

The second implication of costing stock is profit determination. Full cost, in attributing a share of fixed overhead to stock, will result in less of the current period's overhead being capitalized (i.e. treated as an asset) and less being charged (as part of the cost of sales) to the profit and loss account. The full impact of this on profit depends also upon the level of stocks brought forward at the start of the period. Example 2.1 shows how these two alternative approaches can be applied to produce patterns of profits over time which contrast markedly as stocks are first built up and then run down.

These competing bases for stock valuation are well discussed in the literature. The above example is designed merely to emphasize the contrasting consequences of each approach with, in this case, full costing showing a growth in profits and variable costing a marked deterioration. The full cost basis produces higher stock valuations and a pattern of profits over time which are influenced heavily by production levels. In the short run, profits can be improved (through the carry forward of fixed costs in stock) by increasing production and building up stocks. This effect is exaggerated where excess or unused capacity exists and where a proportion of its cost (represented largely by fixed costs) is attached to stock and treated as an asset. The risks and costs associated with this may prove dysfunctional to the firm in the medium term, although profitability rises in the short term. Thus the use of full cost as a basis of stock valuation can motivate inappropriate managerial behaviour. These problems can be mitigated somewhat by the use of a "normal" activity level based on production capacity (see pp. 44–45 for more details) to unitize fixed costs for stock valuation. In contrast, variable costing shows a profit pattern which mirrors sales volume. The level of stockholding does not influence profits. All fixed costs, including

EXAMPLE 2.1
Full v. variable costing for profit measurement

Data:

	Year 1	Year 2	Year 3
Production	160 units	120 units	80 units
Sales	100 units	120 units	140 units
Selling price per unit	£10	£10	£10
Variable cost per unit	£5	£5	£5
Fixed costs	£500	£500	£500

Income statements on a full costing basis

	Year 1 £	£	Year 2 £	£	Year 3 £	£
Sales		1000.00		1200.00		1400.00
Stock (beginning)	—		487.50		550.00	
Cost of goods manufactured	1300.00		1100.00		900.00	
	1300.00		1587.50		1450.00	
Less stock (end)*	487.50		550.00		—	
Cost of sales		812.50		1037.50		1450.00
Profit (Loss)		187.50		162.50		(50.00)

*Stock (end) – assumes FIFO basis. The computation of the profit and loss figures is shown below.

Continued

21

EXAMPLE 2.1
Continued

	Year 1		Year 2	
Variable cost of production	160 units @ £5	= £ 800	120 units @ £5	= £ 600
Fixed cost		= £ 500		= £ 500
Total production cost		£1300		£1100
Unit cost:				
Variable cost	£ 800 ÷ 160	= £5	£ 600 ÷ 120	= £5
Fixed cost	£ 500 ÷ 160	= £3.125	£ 500 ÷ 120	= £4.166
Total unit cost	£1 300 ÷ 160	= £8.125	£1,100 ÷ 120	= £9.166
Stock (end):				
Variable cost	60 @ £5	= £300	60 @ £5	= £300
Fixed cost	60 @ £3.125	= £187.50	60 @ £4.166	= £250
Total cost	60 @ £8.125	= £487.50	60 @ £9.166	= £550

Income statements on a variable costing basis

	Year 1		Year 2		Year 3	
	£	£	£	£	£	£
Sales		1000		1200		1400
Stock (beg.)	—		300		300	
Variable cost of goods manufactured	800		600		400	
	800		900		700	
Less stock (end)*	300		300		—	
Variable cost of sales		500		600		700
Contribution margin		500		600		700
Fixed costs		500		500		500
Profit		—		100		200

*Stock is included at its marginal cost, i.e. 60 units at £5 = £300

the costs of providing capacity for the period, are charged fully in the period's profit and loss account.

Thus the treatment of overhead cost in stock valuation has created one of the great debates in the accounting literature. Although in external reporting standard setters have required full costing, their choice has never been wholly substantiated by either the conceptual or practical arguments relating to this issue.

Decision-making

Economic theory of the firm attributes a central role to unit cost information as a key factor underlying the determination of the level of output. Given a profit-maximizing objective this will occur where unit marginal cost is equal to unit marginal revenue. As marginal cost represents the incremental cost associated with an extra unit of output, the need for an understanding of how costs behave with respect to output volume is emphasized. Thus the separation of overhead into its fixed and variable components is necessary in order to facilitate decisions on whether or not a change in output will increase profits. Furthermore, in order to achieve an equilibrium output the firm should operate at the lowest point on its short-run average cost curve (in the short

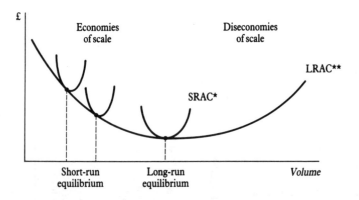

* SHORT-RUN – Technology and equipment of the firm is given.
** LONG-RUN – Technology and equipment of the firm can vary.

FIGURE 2.1

term) and the lowest point on its long-run average cost curve (in the long term). As shown in Figure 2.1, this will involve monitoring full unit costs over time to track the pattern and ascertain where the minimum cost lies.

The unit costs used by economists in output decisions differ from those used by the accountant (and described in Chapter 1). They are based on the notion of opportunity cost, incorporating an imputed charge for the opportunity cost of capital. This extra "cost" represents the return which could have been made had the resources been applied to their most profitable alternative use. In practice this would be effected by computing the cost of capital (see, for example, Brealey and Myers, 1991) of the firm and applying it to the capital employed in the production of the product. The difference between the resultant unit cost and the sales revenue, accountants term residual income, i.e. residual income equals accounting income less (capital employed × cost of capital rate). It can be used as the basis of a decision rule for management: if residual income for a product is positive, then the product is economically viable; if negative it is a drain on the overall profitability of the firm. In practice, residual income is more commonly applied to the measurement of divisional performance (Solomons, 1965; Tomkins, 1973) but provided the capital resources used by a product are identifiable it does also provide a useful basis input to decisions on product output.

While average unit costs provide one economic perspective on product line analysis, incremental costs represent the core accounting contribution to the dynamics of decision making. The latter involve identification of those costs which will change in the future with respect to whatever decision is to be taken. If the decision has a short-run time horizon and requires changing output volumes, then the identification of variable costs should provide the basis for estimating the change in costs. These decisions usually involve alterations to the production mix, the choice of subcontracting out or making units in house; stock level alterations and quoting for work to utilize spare capacity. They have an immediate effect on output levels and consequently on the costs directly affected by output. This will include the variable components of overhead, e.g. the increase or decrease in power costs, maintenance and lubrication caused by the decision. All other costs are considered to be unaffected by the policy selected. Indeed the accountant will be expected to provide this information as a basis for the decision support models, such as break-even or linear programming, which can be used to assist management to assess the financial implications of alternative courses of action.

However, where decisions involve a longer-term impact on the firm, e.g. the permanent abandonment of product lines, the introduction of a new range of products or major modifications to product design or work methods, then the use of the short-run variable cost concept is inappropriate. As the time-scale increases, more and more costs can be considered variable, and eventually if a long enough time perspective is taken all costs may vary and so become relevant to the financial assessment of the decision which is faced. The conventional unitization of indirect costs on the basis of broad overhead rates which at best reveal merely the two fixed and variable components does not therefore contribute much assistance for the longer-term decision. Chapter 3 shows how activity-based costing permits a more detailed analysis of the fixed overhead element of unit cost to enable a clearer view to be taken of why and how it may alter in response to managerial decisions.

Where the decision has medium- to long-run implications for costs (and revenues), the time value of money becomes important and can be taken into account through the use of discounting techniques.

One final decision-making role for unit cost information concerns the setting of prices for the firm's output. The practice of cost-plus pricing has long been attributed to management (Hall and Hitch, 1939), and provides a powerful argument for the importance of this type of information. Current research continues to show that managers value full information which incorporates overheads for pricing decisions (Govindarajan, 1983; Mills, 1988). Although managers do claim to act in this way, it is a practice which clashes somewhat with the idea of price being set by reference to the interaction of supply and demand in the market-place. Machlup (1967) suggested a solution to this dilemma which leaves unit cost information with a central position in the pricing decision. His view was that while managers did take cost as a base point for setting price, the mark-up which they applied to it was not fixed, but varied according to their assessment of the market(s) in which they operated.

Performance measurement

As discussed above, the maximization of profits in the long run requires operations to be directed to the low point on the long-run average cost curve. This implies that full unit cost information should be monitored over time to assess the appropriateness of managerial resourcing and output decisions. Falling unit costs will, at least, indicate progress being made towards the low cost equilibrium point. It will also reflect improvements in the utilization of the resources under management's stewardship, as a unit cost results from the division of inputs (resource costs) by outputs (volumes produced) and as such is simply an inverted productivity measure. Reductions in unit costs can therefore directly reflect management's organization and operation of the business.

The unit cost measure, being ratio derived, can therefore provide a useful time-period comparison if appropriate allowance can be made for inflation. This can be further enhanced as a basis for performance assessment by comparing its pattern over time with the unit costs of other manufacturing plants within the same organization or, to provide a strategic dimension, with those of competing firms. Figure 2.2 shows how this might be done for a six-period comparison between two competitors.

These unit costs show a new entrant (dotted lines) being rebuffed by the established firm (solid lines). Due to cost-based

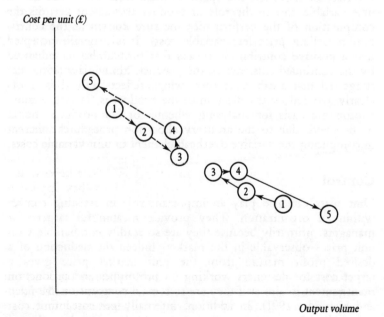

FIGURE 2.2 Unit cost comparisons.

barriers to entry, the new entrant begins at a much higher unit cost and is able (perhaps through effective product differentiation policies) to make inroads into the established firm's market over the first three periods. However, it is not able to achieve the volume of that firm, which responds (possibly with a price cut which it can better afford than the new entrant) in period four and thereafter extends its relative cost advantage by reaping the rewards of expanding output volume.

To enhance this type of benchmarking, unit costs can be segmented by cost element and by the manner in which costs behave (fixed v. variable). This detail provides useful performance feedback, pointing to the source of cost advantages and disadvantages. However, the management accountant has to be innovative and resourceful in estimating the breakdown of competitor costs.

Finally the comparison of full unit costs with unit selling price can provide one piece of evidence which can be used to assess a product's viability. This comparison does give one view of the cost recovery needed in selling price for profits to be made. It must always be borne in mind, however, that full cost information is particular to one volume level and to the arbitrary selection of a variety of allocation and apportionment techniques. The use of unit variable cost in the role of product assessment permits the computation of the performance measure known as the contribution (selling price less variable cost). It is generally accepted that a positive contribution means that profitability is enhanced by the continued existence of the product. Shillinglaw (1963) has suggested that attributable cost, which reflects only those costs clearly avoided by the deletion of the product is, in fact, a more appropriate basis for analysing whether or not products should be dropped, due to the arbitrary allocation procedures inherent in computing the variable overhead element of unit variable costs.

Control

Unit costs can also play an important role in assisting control within an organization. They provide meaningful targets for managers, primarily because they are so readily comparable with unit prices observable in the market. Indeed the deduction of a desired profit margin from the unit market price gives a target cost for designers working on prototypes and production management to aim at if they are to remain competitive (Monden and Hamada, 1991). In addition, internally generated unit cost targets based on experience of past actual costs and work and engineering studies are the basis of unit standard costs which provide a widely used foundation for cost control, particularly in the manufacturing sector (Chow *et al.*, 1988; Lyall *et al.*, 1990). They are normally split into three elements of cost (direct material, direct labour and production overhead) and provide a means of comparing actual costs with expected costs. The variance between these two can be split into those parts attributable to the acquisition and use of the resources, so that higher or lower costs than expected can be traced to those with managerial responsibilities for them (see Chapter 5). Finally, Baxter and Oxenfeldt (1968) have suggested that the phenomenon of cost-plus pricing practice is in fact simply one way in which the management of an organization can exercise some measure of control over events to help ensure the achievement of planned performance. The budget set at the start of the period will include estimated gross profits for all products. From these, the budgeted mark-up on costs can be deduced. If these mark-ups are applied as the "plus" to the actual unit costs derived and reported to management then, provided the budgeted sales volumes are achieved, so will the original budgeted profit.

For all of these important reasons, reliable unit cost information is required by management. It is the cost or management accountant who has the remit to produce it in a suitable format and in a timely fashion.

UNITIZING OVERHEADS: TRADITIONAL PRACTICE

The traditional approach to cost unitization involves the establishment of a documentary based recording system for tracing direct costs to specific product outputs. Thus direct material issues to production will be recorded in a manner which links them at the time of issue to either particular units of output (job or contract costing), batches of output (batch costing) or production runs (process costing). In the case of the latter two cost objects, division of the direct material costs of the batch or production run by the units involved in the batch or production run will give a material unit cost. Direct labour costs can be similarly specifically attached to output through the maintenance of time sheet records by production employees.

In contrast to direct costs, overheads cannot be directly linked to particular outputs and are therefore attributed to production through the application of overhead rates (see Figure 2.3).

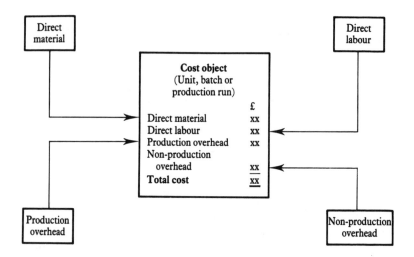

FIGURE 2.3 The components of a product costing system.

The use of production overhead rates involves a two-stage process. First, the overheads are all attributed (through allocation, apportionment and reapportionment) to cost centres (usually production departments or sub-sets of production departments) through which the product output of the organization will pass. Second, a selection is made of a base which reflects the extent to which products consume the resources of the cost centre. This base, which can be directly linked to output, is then used as the basis for attributing each element of product output a proportion of the overhead cost. Figure 2.4 outlines the processes involved.

Example 2.2 illustrates how this process would work in practice.

NON-PRODUCTION OVERHEAD

This category of cost includes a whole range of cost types – distribution, sales, marketing, administration and research and

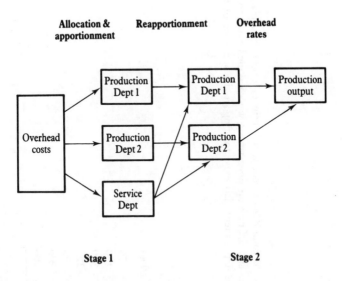

FIGURE 2.4 Production overhead rates.

development. Traditionally, however, non-production overheads have been treated as a single cost pool and attached to products through one global predetermined overhead rate. This is normally based upon the production cost of output sold during the period (see Example 2.3). This approach has the advantages of convenience and low cost, as it uses readily available information, but unless products consume the relevant resources in proportion to their cost of production then it will result in misleading total unit costs.

Given the significance of this class of cost in many organizations, it is important that it is included in unit cost information designed for the purposes (with the exception of stock valuation) outlined at the start of this chapter. These overheads will include both fixed and variable components. Consequently any measurement of unit contribution will be inaccurate if they are excluded and therefore analyses and decisions involving cost/volume/profit, product mix and product retention would be flawed. Likewise

31

EXAMPLE 2.2
Overhead unitization

Structure

Traditional Production Ltd produces cast-iron baths. It has a Pressing department which utilizes a moulding machine and an oven to generate the basic bath shape and enamel it, and a finishing department where skilled workers add fittings and package the bath. A canteen and a Maintenance department also exist to support the activities of these two production departments.

Overheads

Expected annual overhead costs are as follows:

	£000s
Canteen wages & supplies	70
Maintenance wages	130
Depreciation – moulding machine	300
– oven	120
– building	80
Building rent	200
Building heat, light & power (electricity)	100
	1000

Departmental details

	Canteen	Maintenance	Pressing	Finishing
Floor area (sq. m)	1000	1000	6000	2000
Number of employees	5	10	30	10
Estimated usage of maintenance workers' time (hrs)	400	—	2800	1200
Direct labour hours	—	—	50000	25000

Production

The first batch of baths produced in January comprised 500 baths, took 2400 labour hours in Pressing and 800 labour hours in Finishing.

Solution

The objective is to share the £1 million of overhead between the two production departments through which all production will pass so that departmental overhead rates can be used to cost each batch of output. This involves four steps:

1. The direct allocation of certain overheads to particular departments, e.g. the machine depreciation which clearly relates to the Pressing department.
2. The apportionment of certain overheads on a basis reflecting cost usage to the departments, e.g. the building rental on the basis of floor area.

Continued

EXAMPLE 2.2

Continued

3. The reapportionment of the service department costs to the production departments on a basis reflecting their use of the service departments, e.g. the canteen and maintenance costs on the basis of number of employees and maintenance workers' time respectively.

4. The determination of production department overhead rates for the period, i.e. overhead cost ÷ a production characteristic having a strong causal relationship with overhead cost, e.g. the time spent working on a batch by direct labour could be used as the rate denominator in the two departments.

Steps	Basis	Total (£)	Canteen (£)	Maintenance (£)	Pressing (£)	Finishing (£)
1. **Direct allocation:**						
Canteen wages & supplies		70 000	70 000			
Maintenance wages		130 000		130 000		
Depreciation – machine		300 000			300 000	
– oven		120 000			120 000	
2. **Apportionment:**						
Depreciation – building	Floor area	80 000	8 000	8 000	48 000	16 000
Building rental	Floor area	200 000	20 000	20 000	120 000	40 000
Electricity	Floor area	100 000	10 000	10 000	60 000	20 000
Sub-total		1 000 000	108 000	168 000	648 000	76 000

3. Reapportionment of service dept. costs:

		Canteen	Maintenance	Pressing	Finishing
Canteen	No. of employees	−108 000		+81 000	+27 000
Maintenance	Maintenance worker time		−168 000	+117 600	+50 400
A. Total overhead		1 000 000	–	846 600	153 400
B. Direct labour hours		–		50 000	25 000
Departmental overhead rates (A ÷ B)				£16.93	£6.14

Overhead cost of Batch 1

	Pressing	Finishing
Direct labour hours	2,400	800
Overhead rate	£16.93	£6.14
Batch overhead cost	£40 632	£4 912
Overhead cost per unit/bath (÷ 500 units in batch)	£81.26	£9.82

35

EXAMPLE 2.3

Unitizing non-production overhead

	£000s
1. Budgeted annual non-production overhead	10 000
2. Budgeted annual cost of production	40 000

Predetermined non-production overhead rate (1 ÷ 2) <u>£0.25</u> per £
of production cost

∴ Product Z –

Production cost (per unit)	£30.00
Non-production cost (£0.25 × 30)	7.50
Total unit cost	£37.50

---

their omission from unit costs used in pricing decisions or benchmarking would create significant deficiencies.

However, one problematic area of unit costing relates to the research and development component of this class of cost. This is because the research and development cost actually incurred in any period usually relates primarily to new products. As they will only appear in future periods, there is a timing mismatch between R&D incurred and the actual production of any period. If R&D was unitized in its period of incurrence than a year of particularly heavy investment could, where costs were a strong influence on pricing, result in a reduction in competitiveness.

Kaplan (1988) suggeests that it is inappropriate to burden current product costs with the R&D of the next generation of products. This means that the organization will focus on planning its R&D cost recovery over the product life cycle, costs being attributed to the products derived from the R&D activity. This then eliminates the arbitrariness which is brought to the association of R&D cost and output on an accounting period basis, but necessitates careful planning of the financing of this expenditure.

OVERHEAD UNITIZATION: ISSUES ARISING

This example shows the steps taken by management accountants in tackling the problems of unitizing production overheads. The procedures adopted have gradually evolved and have involved a series of judgements on a range of issues which have emerged in this area of costing practice.

Single v. multiple production overhead rates

How many production overhead rates should an organization have? The answer to this question should depend on a cost/benefit analysis of the situation confronting each organization, the costs being driven by the number of rates and the benefits by the utility of the resultant information for management. The latter point will to a large extent be determined by the nature of overhead costs and production output in the organization.

If output consisted of one line of identical units, then a simple averaging by units of output (i.e. one total overhead rate per unit) would be appropriate for producing unit costs. Even in this simple situation it would be desirable to split this rate by production departments if one purpose of producing unit cost information was to identify, for management, where the costs have been incurred, say as a basis for analysing performance over time.

Two other reasons can also be put forward for an organization having more than simply one global overhead rate:

1. Product outputs are different and make different demands on the resources of different production centres, e.g.

	Production Department 1	*Production Department 2*	*Total*
Production overhead	£28 000	£72 000	£100 000
Direct labour hours	4 000 hrs	6 000 hrs	10 000 hrs
Overhead rates	£7 per hr	£12 per hr	£10 per hr
Product A	10 hrs	40 hrs	50 hrs
Product B	25 hrs	25 hrs	50 hrs

Products A and B each involve a total of 50 direct labour hours of work, and therefore if a single total overhead rate was in use each product would attract exactly the same amount of overhead cost (50 hrs × £10 = £500). However, product A spends relatively more time in the department (2) with the higher overhead rate, and because of this it consumes more overhead cost. It requires the application of departmental rates to reflect this in the overhead costings:

				£
Product A	– Dept 1	10 hrs × £7		70
	– Dept 2	40 hrs × £12		480
				550

Product B	– Dept 1	25 hrs × £7		175
	– Dept 2	25 hrs × £12		300
				475

2. The overhead costs of the organization are not homogeneous in respect of a causal relationship with one production characteristic, i.e. the overhead rate denominator, e.g:

	Production Department 6
Overhead costs – machine-related	£120 000
– labour-related	£ 80 000
	£200 000
Direct labour hours	2 000 hours
Machine hours	500 hours

	Direct labour hrs	Machine hrs
Product X	10 hrs	5 hrs
Product Y	20 hrs	2 hrs

In this situation the single total rate for Production Department 6 would be £100 per hour (£200 000 ÷ 2 000 hrs) when based on direct labour hours and £400 per hour when based on machine hours. This would cost the products for overheads as follows:

Direct labour hours

Machine hours

Product X 10 hrs × £100 = £1 000   5 hrs × £400 =   £2 000

Product Y 20 hrs × £100 = £2 000   2 hrs × £400 =   £ 800

However, these total rates ignore the heterogeneity of the costs within the total pool. Forty per cent of overheads are dependent on labour time and the other 60 per cent on machine time. It is only when this is recognized and the total overhead cost pool is split into homogeneous subpools that the use of overhead rates becomes rational. Thus to produce coherent overhead rates in this situation, Production Department 6 should be split into two cost centres, one based on machine-related overhead and the other on worktime-related overhead. This would result in the following overhead costings:

	Production Department 6	
	Machine-related overhead	*Worktime-related overhead*
Costs	£120 000	£80 000
Overhead rate denominator	500 machine hours	2 000 direct labour hours
Overhead rates	£240 per mach. hr.	£40 per direct labour hour

Product X: £1 600 = 5 hrs × £240 = £1 200 + 10 hrs × £40 = £400

Product Y: £1 280 = 2 hrs × £240 = £480 + 20 hrs × £40 = £800

In most organizations of any complexity, where labour and capital resources are combined in the production of a range of outputs, the need to segregate overheads into multiple homogeneous cost pools and have separate overhead rates for each will be apparent. The analysis of overhead costs in terms of homogeneity may lead to a variety of different bases being used for overhead rates. Direct labour hours (or direct labour cost for convenience) and machine hours are most common, but others could include prime cost (where more costly units cause more overhead), direct material cost or size (where the overhead pool relates to handling or storage) or simply units of output (where each unit passing through the cost centre causes the same demand for overhead resource). To neglect this issue can lead to significantly inaccurate unit costs. Indeed it is just such a neglect which has contributed to the emergence and growth of activity-based costing (see Chapter 4).

Pre-determined overhead rates

Overhead rates are normally set on an annual basis and are used to cost production work when it is still in the manufacturing process (work in progress) and when it emerges as finished output. If this information is to be produced within a reasonable time-scale, then the rate established for any year has to be available for use from the start of the year to cost the initial work undertaken.

This precludes the use of actual figures to compute the rate, as these would only be available after the end of the year. Thus, in practice, overhead rates are based on budgeted or predetermined figures for the year in question. The rate is therefore a best estimate, and the overhead component of the resultant unit costs should be viewed in this light. Of course the realism of the predetermined figures can be monitored and assessed throughout the year by comparing the actual overheads incurred with the original budget (numerator of the rate) and with the amounts being applied to production which will also be determined by the actual volumes of the selected base (denominator of the rate). The use of the predetermined rate can therefore result in an overcosting (overabsorption) or an undercosting (underabsorption) of output. Example 2.4 illustrates how this can occur.

Overhead rate denominator level

As the above example illustrates, the level at which the overhead rate denominator is set will be a major determinant of the resultant unit overhead cost. The denominator is normally based upon some aspect of production activity (e.g. direct labour hours or machine hours). Thus when the rate is established for a period of a year any seasonal variation is eliminated, the same rate being applied throughout the year. However, where the production output of an organization is growing or shrinking, or exhibits a cyclical pattern of output, then considerable variation may occur in the basis for computing the level of the selected denominator from year to year.

This does highlight the importance of output volumes as a determinant of unit costs and accounts for the variety of practice in the area (Purdy, 1965). When actual annual volumes are used in a cyclical situation, then in the recessionary years unit overhead costs will be higher, as the costs of unused capacity are spread over the low levels of production. This may render the unit cost information of dubious value for certain purposes. First, if it is used in pricing it may lead to rising prices which will exaggerate the recessionary effects on volumes and lead to a vicious cycle of falling output and rising unit costs. Second, the value of stock in recessionary years will include some of the costs of unused capacity. Few accountants would support the treatment of such costs as assets. A more prudent approach would be to treat them as period costs and write them off directly against income in the period in which they occur.

These drawbacks associated with the use of the expected actual output volume as the overhead rate denominator have led to the advocacy of long-term average volumes or capacity-based volumes for unitizing overheads for pricing and stock valuation respectively. Example 2.5 shows how these concepts would be applied.

Apportionment and reapportionment

Where costs are not specifically attributable to the individual cost centres upon which overhead rates are based, some form of apportionment takes place. As Example 2.2 showed, this involves finding a suitable measurement base which reflects how the cost centres consume the relevant resource. Thus floor area may provide a reasonable indication of how each production department consumes electricity for heating and lighting a factory. In this instance the basis chosen should represent a reasonable proxy for the costs obtained should electricity consumption be metered exactly.

Where service cost centres exist, their costs also require reapportionment to the cost centres used for overhead rates. Certain additional complications are created by this requirement, particularly where the service centres provide reciprocal services. In Example 2.2 this problem was ignored. Although Maintenance did work for the canteen and the canteen was used by maintenance workers, no account was taken of these reciprocal services. The service centre costs were simply apportioned to the production departments. Where the usage of service centre resource by production departments differs markedly and the costs of the reciprocal services are dissimilar (i.e. they do not simply cross-compensate), then ignoring them could lead to material costing inaccuracies.

Example 2.2 ignored this problem, with the service department costs being directly reapportioned to the production departments.

EXAMPLE 2.4
Predetermined overhead rates

Predetermined annual rate	*Absorbed by annual production*	*Actual annual overhead incurred*
$\dfrac{\text{Budgeted overhead cost}}{\text{Budgeted direct labour hours}}$	Predetermined rate	× Actual direct labour hours worked in producing 1992 actual output	Taken from ledger records of 1992
$= \dfrac{£500\,000}{100\,000\ \text{hrs}}$	£5.00	× 90 000 hrs	
$= £5.00$ per direct labour hour	$= £450\,000$		£350 000

Here the use of the predetermined rate has resulted in an overabsorption of £100 000. This is a relatively large amount, being 29 per cent of the actual overhead of the year. If overhead were a significant proportion of total costs it would certainly cast some doubt on the accuracy of unit costs and might, for example, lead to overpricing where costs are used to influence selling price. In order to minimize over/underabsorptions, the process of absorption is usually closely

42

monitored, at least on a monthly basis, and where appropriate the rate can be revised to a more realistic level. Monitoring should encompass an assessment of why the rate is not proving to be accurate. The two possible reasons are inaccurate prediction of the numerator or denominator of the rate. From the information given, the underabsorption can be attributed to each of these factors:

1. Volume of work (as measured by the direct labour hours denominator)

Actual overhead absorbed =	90 000 hrs × £5.00	£450 000
Estimated absorption =	100 000 hrs × £5.00	£500 000
Underabsorption		50 000

2. Spending on overheads

Actual spend	£350 000
Expected spend (budget)	£500 000
Overabsorption	150 000

Thus the feedback to the rate-setter can identify an overestimation in terms of the number of hours to be worked during the year and an underestimation of the ability of staff to control the level of overhead spend.

EXAMPLE 2.5

Actual v. average v. capacity bases for overhead rates

Year	Expected actual volumes (Direct labour hrs)	Long-run average volume (Direct labour hrs)	Capacity volume provided (Direct labour hrs)
1	100 000	90 000	130 000
2	110 000	90 000	130 000
3	90 000	90 000	130 000
4	80 000	90 000	130 000
5	70 000	90 000	130 000

Annual expected overhead cost £900 000

Overhead rate options:

Year	Expected actual		Long-run average		Capacity provided	
	Rate per DLH	Overhead absorbed (£)	Rate per DLH	Overhead absorbed (£)	Rate per DLH	Overhead absorbed (£)
1	£9.00	900000	£10.00	1000000	£6.92	692000
2	£8.18	900000	£10.00	1100000	£6.92	761200
3	£10.00	900000	£10.00	900000	£6.92	622800
4	£11.25	900000	£10.00	800000	£6.92	553600
5	£12.86	900000	£10.00	700000	£6.92	484000

The use of an expected actual base for the overhead rate ensures that the actual overhead cost of £900000 is fully absorbed by production each year. However, it will also produce considerable variability in the overhead rate and in the firm's annual unit costs. The short-run (annual) impact of volume changes on cost is emphasized. In contrast, the average basis ensures that overheads are only absorbed by production in the long run (five-year period). There are overabsorptions in years 1 and 2 and underabsorptions in years 4 and 5. The overhead rate, however, is constant, lending a stability to unit costs over the period. If, for example, pricing were related to costs then overheads would provide no cause for variation. This would benefit customers through reducing supply price uncertainty, but could lead to problems in years 1 and 2 if competitors determined costs on an actual basis and priced accordingly.

Finally, the use of capacity volume provides both stability, a prudent basis for stock valuation and the potential for costs which will aid pricing competitiveness. However, it also means a considerable underabsorption of cost each year. If this is not recovered from customers, profitability and viability may be threatened.

EXAMPLE 2.6
The step method of reapportionment

| | Service centres | | Production centres | |
	Canteen £	Maintenance £	Pressing £	Finishing £
Costs	108 000	168 000	648 000	76 000
Reapportionment of canteen (basis – number of employees in other centres)	−108 000	+21 600 (20%)	+64 800 (60%)	+21 600 (20%)
		189 600	712 800	97 600
Reapportionment of maintenance (basis – hours worked for other centres)	—	−189 600	+132 720 (70%)	+56 880 (30%)
		—	845 520	154 480

The step method or the simultaneous equation method can be used to take service centre reciprocal services into account; their application to the data of Example 2.2 is illustrated below.

The step method

One service department is chosen first and its costs reapportioned to all other user cost centres (both production and service). Then another service department is chosen and its costs are reapportioned to all other user cost centres except the first selected service department. By taking each service department in turn, all service department costs are eventually reapportioned to production departments. This approach clearly only partially takes account of service department reciprocal services. Once a reapportionment has occurred, the department concerned cannot be burdened with the cost of the use which it makes of those service departments which have still to be reapportioned, e.g. the service provided by maintenance to the canteen is ignored (see Example 2.6).

The order of reapportionment is therefore important in minimizing the effects of this limitation. Those service departments which make little or no use of the others (and therefore are due to receive no cost reapportionment) and those which provide little or no service to the others (and whose reapportionment is immaterial) should be reapportioned first, and thereafter the level of costs in the centre which pertain to other service centres provides a reasonable rule for ordering their reapportionment.

Simultaneous equations

This approach takes account of the reciprocal services in a less arbitrary manner, as it recognizes and takes account of all existing cross-relationships between the service centres. Basically the unknowns, i.e. the total costs of each service centre, are first identified by solving the appropriate simultaneous equations. They are then reapportioned on appropriate bases. The process which can be applied to situations where multiple service departments exist is illustrated in Example 2.7, again using the simple data from Example 2.2.

Clearly these methods of reapportionment are more rigorous than the direct approach. They are also more time-consuming and costly to implement. Therefore, in essence, the decision to employ them will depend on the importance of unit cost information to the organization and on whether or not their application results in unit cost information which is materially

EXAMPLE 2.7

Reapportionment by simultaneous equations

Let A = Full canteen cost to be reapportioned
Let B = Full maintenance cost to be reapportioned

$$A = £108\,000 + \frac{400^\star}{4400}\,B$$

$$B = £168\,000 + \frac{10^{\star\star}}{50}\,A$$

★Based on number of hours worked by maintenance staff in user departments
★★Based on number of employees in user departments

Solution:

$$A = £125\,555$$

$$B = £193\,111$$

Reapportionment

| | Service centres | Production centres | |
| | | Pressing | Finishing |
	£	£	£
Costs:			
Canteen (basis – no. of employees)	—	648 000	76 000
Maintenance (basis – hours worked)	125 555	75 333 (60%)[+]	25 111 (20%)[+]
	193 111	123 591 (64%)[+]	52 140 (27%)[+]
		846 924	153 251

[+]These represent the proportions of the basis selected which pertain to the production departments. Thus in this case another 20 per cent of canteen cost pertains to maintenance and the other 9 per cent of maintenance to canteen.

EXAMPLE 2.8
Overhead unitization flexibility

JUDGEMENTAL AREAS

Single v. multiple rates	Overhead rate denominator	Service centre reapportionment	Overhead apportionment bases
SAY four possibilities	SAY three possibilities	SAY three possibilities	SAY six possibilities

Possible alternative unit overhead costs = $4 \times 3 \times 3 \times 6 = \underline{216}$

different from that produced in a less sophisticated and costly way. In the above example, the more rigorous approaches differ little from the results of direct reapportionment.

COMMENTARY

The existence of multiple products or services sharing the use of certain factors of production is a common organizational characteristic and one which creates the need for a system of overhead allocation and apportionment. The degree of association (and hence traceability) of the cost of these factors to the product will vary, but for many general costs the linkages will be somewhat tenuous. While the procedures described above may have had some measure of justification at the time and in the context of their development in the past (Johnson and Kaplan, 1987a), they have come under increasing criticism in recent years. Moreover their defence has proved difficult, as they are based on a number of often subjective judgements between competing alternatives, none of which can be considered "correct".

This creates an inherent flexibility which renders any unit overhead cost information of dubious quality for, as Example 2.8 illustrates, from the same basic costing situation the same total overhead cost can be spread over output in many different ways. In an organization of any complexity the unit overhead cost for a product is an unattainable figure. Only one unit overhead cost from among a wide range of possibilities can be obtained, and it is dependent on the particular choices made by accountants in each of the judgemental areas.

Thus any unit overhead cost may well merit being treated with a certain amount of scepticism, as it is only one from among many possibilities. This stems from the fact that the judgemental measurement decisions outlined above involve the selection of a whole series of surrogates to represent the pattern of consumption of resources by individual products. Assessment of these at a conceptual level is, of course, always possible and this can, and should, be reinforced by some regular empirical testing perhaps for statistical correlation (e.g. between the overhead rate denominator and the cost centre costs) or, at least, by consultation and vetting of procedures by those involved in the underlying operational processes. Where the output is used for performance assessment and control, consistency and uniformity of selections both over time and across subjects for comparison are desirable.

The introduction to this chapter outlined some of the purposes of unit cost information. It is these which may underlie the demand for cost allocations necessary to unitize overheads. Nevertheless, it is widely accepted that the questionable nature of these allocations does frequently render the end result of dubious value (Thomas, 1974; Biddle and Steinberg, 1984). However, Zimmerman (1979) has proposed some further justifications for the practice of allocation. He suggests that the allocation of fixed overheads might represent a proxy for unobservable costs associated with the cost object; for example, the opportunity costs associated with the commitment of resources to the manufacture of a product.

In addition, the allocation of overheads may play a role in the principal/agent relationship which exists between superior and subordinate managers within an organization. For example, a product manager may be motivated to monitor and influence the perquisite consumption of senior management and indeed service managers, if costs associated with them are included in the product unit costs which are used in controlling and assessing their performance. Given the arbitrariness of many of the procedures used and the lack of suitability of full unit cost information for decision making, the continuing demand for it from management renders the question of the motivation for overhead unitization one which is worthy of further investigation.

DISCUSSION TOPICS

1. Discuss how the economist's and the accountant's concepts of unit cost differ.
2. Which of the following types of cost should be legitimately included in stock valuation?
   — period costs;
   — fixed costs;
   — costs of inefficiency;
   — costs of idle capacity;
   — general management.
3. Do you think a firm can ever recognize when it has achieved its equilibrium unit cost at the minimum point on its long-run cost curve?
4. How accurately can a firm estimate the unit costs of its closest competitors? (See, for example, L. Jones, 1988.)

5. List the arbitrary classes of decision which have to be made in a complex organization where a traditional approach is being used to generate full unit costs.
6. Normal activity is only a useful notion for the static firm. Discuss.
7. Unit cost information is irrelevant for "price takers". Discuss.

3

The Unitization of Overhead: an Activity-Based Approach

THE MOTIVATION FOR ACTIVITY-BASED COSTING

Many of the techniques of overhead unitization described in the preceding chapter have been in use for the best part of a century (Solomons, 1968). Indeed, cost accountancy was one of the few aspects of business organization which exhibited little evidence of significant change during this period. Thus the context in which the traditional approaches to overhead costing had been developed changed, and certainly by the 1980s many managers and accountants regarded at least the overhead component of unit costs with some suspicion (CBI/Develin & Partners, 1990; Innes and Mitchell, 1991a). In addition, several academics produced highly critical reviews focusing on the use of convenient rather than appropriate means for unitizing overhead (Kaplan, 1984; Johnson and Kaplan, 1987a; Shank and Govindarajan, 1988; Cooper, 1989).

Three major factors contributed to the doubts which were expressed about traditional overhead costing: the growth of overhead cost, the changing nature of overhead cost, and the diminution of direct labour as a proportion of total cost.

Growth of overhead cost

Overhead cost had grown both in absolute terms and in terms of its relative significance within the cost structure of many firms (Develin & Partners, 1990). Overhead in many sectors is now the single most important cost element. This increase in importance is attributable to automation, which results in the transfer of cost from the direct labour to the production overhead category and to the growth in marketing and selling costs designed to meet the challenge of intensifying international competition. This growth has imbued the methods of overhead cost unitization with the potential to significantly affect the pattern of unit costs within organizations.

The nature of overhead cost

The nature of overhead cost has changed from the type of cost which supported particular volumes of production (e.g. those linked to the provision of production facilities and the power requirements of manufacturing) to the type which supports an increasing complexity, diversity, economy and quality of production. It is these latter factors, rather than merely product volume growth, which underlie the increase in overhead cost in many modern organizations.

The enhancement of manufacturing flexibility, the increasing role of design and launch of new products coupled with the changes necessitated by product life-cycle reductions, the expansion of product range and customization, the minimization of stock holdings and the investment needed to develop higher-quality competitive products have all been evident in contemporary businesses seeking "world class" manufacturer status. All of these developments create demand for the type of extra resource which gives rise to overhead. Miller and Vollman (1985) view these changes in terms of the types of transaction which have to be undertaken within these organizations and which therefore have to be resourced. They have identified four classes of transaction:

1. *Logistical transactions* These transactions involve the efficient movement and tracking of materials in, through and out of the production process.
2. *Balancing transactions* These transactions involve matching resources with the increasingly complex demands of the modern, flexible production operation. These resources must be acquired and made ready and available where and when they are needed.

3. *Quality transactions* These transactions involve ensuring that output conforms with established specifications which will meet market expectations.
4. *Change transactions* These transactions emanate from the need to be flexible, particularly in response to changes in customer demand. They include dealing with the implications of design, scheduling, supply and production method changes.

It is the growth in volume of these transactions which drives up overhead cost but hopefully also delivers benefits in the form of efficient, flexible and competitive operations.

Direct labour trend

Direct labour has fallen both absolutely and as a proportion of total cost. This trend has tended to occur in organizations mentioned above which are seeking "world class" status. Some electronic sector examples are contained in Innes and Mitchell (1990) and Cooper and Kaplan (1991) which show direct labour as low as 5 per cent or less of total cost. This is significant, as it compounds the inaccuracies of using a traditional labour hour basis for overhead unitization. This is because product volume related bases are traditionally used, with direct labour cost or direct labour hours the most popular of these. When direct labour shrinks to the sorts of level mentioned above and overhead cost increases, the rate per direct labour hour quickly rises, often to abnormally high levels with rates which are hundreds or even thousands of per cent of the related direct labour cost (see Example 3.1).

In situations like these the accuracy of the overhead component of product cost will be highly sensitive to the reliability of the measurement of direct labour cost and to the suitability of direct labour as the base for the rate. The changes in the composition of overhead described above do, in fact, raise serious doubts as to the base's suitability and thus on the validity of its widespread perpetuation in practice. It is primarily a volume-related variable, and as such it is designed for situations where product volume is the major determinant of overhead cost. Where other causal factors are more important, then an alternative basis will be required.

The limitations of traditional overhead costing have been increasingly exposed by changes in the importance and composition of the overhead cost element. These have stemmed from developing production and organizational policies designed to meet changing customer demands in the increasingly competitive international

EXAMPLE 3.1

The impact of direct labour cost reduction on overhead rates

	Relative %				
	Year 1 %	*Year 2* %	*Year 3* %	*Year 4* %	*Year 5* %
(1) Direct material cost	40	40	40	40	40
(2) Direct labour cost	30	20	10	5	2
(3) Production overhead	30	40	50	55	58
	100	100	100	100	100
Overhead rate based on direct labour cost ((3) ÷ (2))	100%	200%	500%	1 100%	2 900%

market-place. These changes have frequently elicited little response from the management accountant, who has continued with the overhead costing system developed in an earlier era. However, since the mid-1980s there have been signs of the emergence of an alternative approach aimed at overcoming the problems of traditional overhead costing.

THE ORIGINS OF ACTIVITY-BASED COSTING

The basic concept of an activity-based approach to costing has existed in the accounting literature for a considerable time. Horngren (1990) attributes an ABC philosophy to the work done on distribution and selling overhead in the 1950s, and indeed has argued that if the basic ideas of conventional costing texts – homogeneity of cost centre costs and the selection of rate denominators which have a close causal relationship with the costs – were logically applied, then the result would in many instances be extremely similar to the ABC systems which emerged in the 1980s. Some of the techniques of zero-based budgeting are based on activity analysis (e.g. Stowich, 1976) and Solomons (1968) explores the need to obtain a reasonably accurate indication of the differing factors driving overhead as a basis for more reliable variance computations. Staubus (1971) actually coins the phrase "activity costing" and outlines its application in theoretical terms.

However, a direct link between this literature and the operational ABC systems which emerged in the 1980s has not been established. Rather, the first reported ABC systems emerged as the creations of management accountants working in large American organizations with acute experience of the above problems of traditional overhead costing. While practical ABC systems originated from industrial management accountants, two academics – Robin Cooper and Robert Kaplan – from the Graduate School of Business Administration, Harvard University, can be credited with its codification into a coherent framework and its dissemination through a series of case studies and articles (Cooper and Kaplan, 1991a). It has proved to be a popular approach, quickly gathering great interest from practitioners, consultants and other academics. Indeed in 1991 Innes and Mitchell found that almost half of the respondents to a UK CIMA member survey worked for organizations which were at least considering the implementation of ABC, although at the time of writing relatively few had actually committed themselves to its adoption. Table 3.1 lists some of the larger UK-based organizations where ABC is being applied.

ABC BASICS

Activity-based product costing systems are most appropriate where overhead is a relatively important cost element, where it is primarily transaction (see above) rather than output volume determined and where there is a diversity of product lines on offer. It is where these conditions hold that ABC is most likely to produce materially different product costs which will more

Table 3.1 Some examples of ABC users in the UK.

British Aerospace (defence)	Guinness (drinks)
Hewlett Packard (electronics)	DHL (couriers)
IBM (electronics)	Norwich Union (insurance)
Black & Decker (tools)	Lucas Industries (engineering)
Royal Bank of Scotland (banking)	Nissan Yamato (cars)
Cummins Engines (engineering)	Severn Trent Water (water)

Source: Based on ABC Software advertising and on conference presentations by staff of the above firms.

accurately reflect the manner in which resources have been consumed by products.

The basic structure of an activity-based costing system is akin to that for traditional overhead unitization, in that it is two-stage, the first involving the pooling of the overhead and the second involving the use of rates to attach the overhead to production output (see Figure 3.1).

However, in Stage 1 the pooling is based on the activities which have consumed resources and given rise to overhead cost rather than on the basis of production departments or centres. The activities selected are based upon classes of transaction such as those described in the Miller and Vollmann study mentioned earlier. Frequently these will run across the formal departmental boundaries of an organization. For example, purchasing activity will be found in R&D, procurement, customer liaison, administration, finance and stores. In Stage 2 the rates for application to products are based on a series of cost drivers which indicate how each product has made demands on the various activities. The cost drivers are normally based upon the transactions underlying

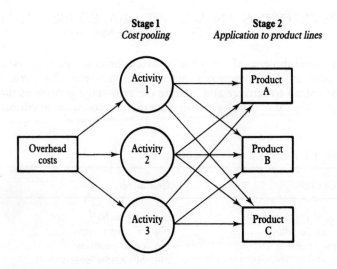

FIGURE 3.1 The basic structure of an activity-based product costing system.

each activity. The rates are computed by dividing the activity cost for a period by the cost driver volume for the same period. Thus to apply the rate, cost driver volumes must be collected for each product line. The underlying philosophy reflected in this process is that activities consume resources and products consume activities. Table 3.2 shows some examples of typical activities which might be used and corresponding cost drivers which might be used as components of an ABC system.

It should be noted that ABC focuses on those overheads which are not driven by product volume. It is quite possible that in many organizations volume-driven overheads will also exist, and these should continue to be attached to output in the appropriate conventional manner (e.g. on the basis of labour hours or machine hours).

While much of the literature on ABC focuses on production overheads, it is an approach which can be applied to all overhead costs. Roth and Sims (1991) outline an application to warehousing, Cooper and Kaplan (1991a) in the Winchell Lighting Case illustrate its application to distribution channel cost, while Reeve (1992) demonstrates how it can attach sales and administration overheads by utilizing cost drivers such as order volume, order complexity and customer volume.

DEVELOPING AN ACTIVITY-BASED PRODUCT COSTING SYSTEM

The development of an activity-based product costing system requires a logical approach which will generate the necessary information to achieve and operate the two-stage process outlined above. This will involve the management accountant in consider-

Table 3.2 Activities and cost drivers.

Activity	*Cost driver*
Material procurement	No. of purchase orders
Material handling	No. of movements
Quality control	No. of inspections
Engineering services	No. of change orders
Maintenance	No. of breakdowns
Line set-up	No. of set-ups

able investigation, data gathering and processing and professional judgements at each of the several steps which are explored below.

Step 1: Profiling the activities

For most businesses this will involve adopting a new perspective on what is actually going on within the organization. Formal organization charts tend to have a traditional functional orientation which is traversed by many activities. Thus a new analysis is usually required to uncover Miller and Vollman's (1985) "hidden factory".

In order to ensure a comprehensive analysis it is necessary to have a sound foundation for the work. One approach is to use a physical map of the work location in order to provide a basis upon which all activities can be identified. The purpose of each space on the map can be ascertained. This can be facilitated by also accounting for all of the staff on the payroll in particular map locations. Thus the facility and labour resource available can be used to, at least, obtain a reliable preliminary outline of both the mainstream and support activities (see Figure 3.2). With the exception of direct production activities, they may all be susceptible to an activity-based approach to unitization.

This may then provide a good foundation for a more detailed activity analysis. In order to do this, those actually involved in each area must be consulted. This is normally done by conducting interviews with a range of staff members and/or having staff fill in a one-off "time sheet" detailing how their time is spent. Reliable information is needed at this stage, otherwise the whole ABC edifice will be built on sand. Moreover, this can be a sensitive step, especially if there is any suggestion that data gathered could be used to cut costs. One of the few reported cases of ABC failure (Robinson, 1989) occurred within an organization where the staff viewed it as a precursor to the selection of redundancies and therefore failed to provide reliable information.

In order to improve the presentation of information from the interviews and to assist in its analysis, Morrow and Hazell (1992) suggest the construction of activity maps, with a basic structure as shown in Figure 3.3. They provide a convenient basis for gathering together the set of activities in a manner which facilitates an understanding of where activities are located, how they are carried out and how the constituent parts link together. The map thus highlights the elements involved in each activity and their timing, which also gives an indication of the labour cost involved.

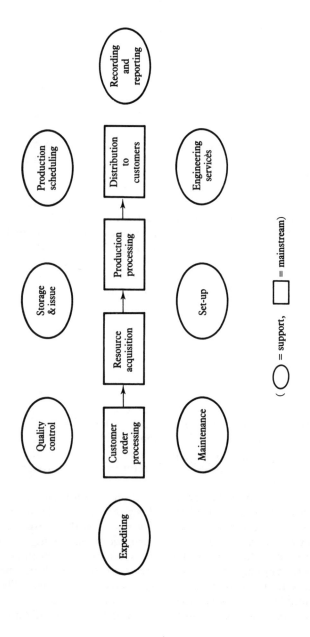

FIGURE 3.2 Activity outline.

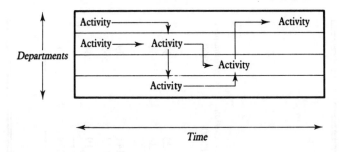

FIGURE 3.3 Activity map structure.

The end result of this work is to produce an inventory of activities which, among other uses, can help in the design of the costing system. This requires the management accountant's judgement to ensure that a suitable level of aggregation is selected. It is activities rather than actions or tasks that have ultimately to be identified, otherwise the data will become more akin to that of a time and motion study. The size and complexity of the organization will be a major determinant of the number of activity pools.

In some of the earliest American cases several hundred activity poolings were used, while in more recent cases more rationalization has occurred to produce a smaller set, often limited to under twenty cost pools. The design of this aspect of the system will also depend on the nature and choice of cost drivers.

Step 2: Pooling the activity costs

Next the selected activities have to be costed. This can be conveniently combined with the previous stage – for example, by using interviews to collect data on staff time involvement and the other resources (e.g. equipment) used to carry out activities. Here the issue of cost apportionment is likely to be relevant. While many costs may be directly attributable to activities, others will not, e.g. staff costs relating to employees who contribute to more than one activity but for whom work time records are not available, equipment which is not dedicated to one activity, and facilities (e.g. buildings) shared by several activities. If these costs

EXAMPLE 3.2
Activity cost profiling

Basic analysis   **Detailed analysis**

Activities	Cost £ million	Sub-Activities	Total cost £000s	Staff costs £000s	Occupancy costs £000s	Depreciation £000s	Consumables £000s
Set-up	8.6						
Maintenance	13.2	Supplier vetting	1066	895	94	23	54
		Prepare purchase agreements	1551	1202	221	24	104
Purchasing	9.4	Supplier liaison	993	765	48	141	39
		Order processing	4130	2675	793	103	559
Production control	3.9	Order expediting	1660	1109	268	19	264
			9400	6646	1424	309	1021
Quality control	4.2						

are included (and they must be, if full unit cost information is the objective) then the arbitrariness associated with apportionment will also violate the ABC process. The clear identification of apportioned costs at the level of product cost is therefore an attribute which should perhaps be built into the ABC system.

The output of this step will be a costing profile (see Example 3.2) of a level of detail which will provide a new perspective on costs, one which exposes what has been done with acquired resources. Management can then assess the cost *vis-à-vis* the value of each activity and can monitor these costs over time and possibly between organizational sub-units. Moreover, this type of cost profiling provides a basis for various types of cost management described in the following chapter.

Ultimately the degree of cost pool segmentation will determine the level of detail of the system. The use of sub-activity pools (see Example 3.2) will allow an increased visibility of costs and usually an enhancement in the homogeneity of the pool. However it will also mean the collection of considerably more data and make the system more costly to establish and operate.

Step 3: Selecting cost drivers

The costs of any activity cost pool will be influenced by a variety of factors, ranging from inflation to staff quality to work organization. While all such factors could be viewed as "driving" cost in ABC, the term "cost driver" is reserved for those factors which reflect the volume of work throughput of the activity. This will be driven by the output demands placed on the activity by other activities including the production of specific product lines. In many instances the cost driver will be measured in terms of the volume of transactions (Miller and Vollman, 1985) undertaken.

Interviews with local management are normally used to "tease out" the activity cost drivers. The questions asked should be designed to elicit the work demands placed on the activity and the sources of that demand, e.g.:

- What services does this activity provide?
- Who receives these services?
- Why do you require X staff?
- What might cause you to require more/less staff?
- Why does over/idle time exist?

Alternative cost drivers will frequently emerge for each activity pool. This can be an indication that the pool can in fact be segmented, with a different driver appropriate to each part. Alternatively the drivers may reflect different attributes of the activity workload, and here an assessment is necessary. This can be done subjectively by taking the advice of those involved in the work, or more objectively through statistical analysis. However, the identification of a statistical correlation between two variables is not, in itself, absolute proof that a causal relationship exists between them. This is significant, for if no causal relationship exists then the future viability of the link is questionable and the supposed independent variable is of limited use for influencing or managing the cost pool concerned (Geitzman, 1991). The need to back statistical procedures with on-the-ground analysis is therefore quite apparent.

Ideally the pooled activity costs should each be homogeneous and in terms of their cost levels being explained by the selected cost driver. In practice, the complexities of cost incurrence will limit the extent to which this is achievable. Moreover the situation should be reviewed regularly to ensure that original choices continue to be merited.

In practice three different types of cost driver have emerged:

1. *Pure activity output volume* This can occur where the basic transactions of the activity are identical in terms of their resource demands. For example, the number of purchase orders could be used as a cost driver for procurement activity costs where the work required to make each purchase order is highly similar.

2. *Activity/output volume/complexity* This can occur where the basic transactions of the activity differ in terms of their resource demands. If a UK-based organization purchased from several different countries, the time and effort involved in each might differ considerably due to the extra administration work involved in buying overseas. For example, if purchases were made in the UK, Germany, USA and Japan, then purchase orders by location could be given an approximate weighting to reflect the resources used in making the respective orders (column (3), Example 3.3). In this way different order costs are distinguished and thus their costs are more accurately associated with product lines.

3. *Situational* This basis can be used where an underlying situational factor can be identified as the key factor determining the workload of the activity. If, for example, the existence of a large number of suppliers was a fundamental determinant of the resources required by purchasing then the number of

---

EXAMPLE 3.3

The weighted purchase order volume cost driver

(1) Order location	(2) No. of orders	(3) Resource usage weighting	(4) Weighted order volume
UK	200 000	10	2 000 000
Germany	50 000	15	750 000
USA	30 000	25	750 000
Japan	10 000	50	500 000
			4 000 000

Procurement overhead = say, £10 000 000

Cost driver rate (£10 000 000 ÷ 4 000 000) = £2.5 per weighted order

Purchase order costs:

UK	(10 × £2.5) =	£ 25.00
Germany	(15 × £2.5) =	£ 37.50
USA	(25 × £2.5) =	£ 62.50
Japan	(50 × £2.5) =	£125.00

---

suppliers could be used as the cost driver. This would be particularly appropriate where supplier vetting and liaison were major components of the cost pool or where the proliferation of suppliers was a problem upon which management wished to focus attention.

Step 4: Cost driver rate application

The attribution of the pooled activity costs to products is effected by the use of the cost driver rates. In order to do this it is necessary to establish a system which will permit the identification of cost driver volumes associated with each production run (process costing), batch (batch costing), contract (contract costing) or job (job costing). The facility with which this can be done will be one of the criteria used in the cost driver selection process. The result will be a unit cost which shows in detail the composition of the overhead element and signals (through the cost driver measure) the factors which underly the consumption of resource (see Example 3.4).

EXAMPLE 3.4

ABC unit cost

	Total cost Month 8 production of Product 2 (10 000 units) £000s	Unit cost (÷ 10 000 units) £
Direct material	280	28.0
Direct labour	50	5.0
Volume related overhead:		
(i) 5 000 direct labour hours @ £12	60	6.0
(ii) 1 000 machine hours @ £80	80	8.0
Activity related overhead:		
(i) 80 inspections @ £500	40	4.0
(ii) 10 set ups @ £200	20	2.0
(iii) 600 material movements @ £20	12	1.2
(iv) 40 change orders @ £1 000	40	4.0
(v) 300 purchase orders @ £60	18	1.8
	600	60.0

ACTIVITY-BASED PRODUCT COSTING: AN EXAMPLE

The application of the above procedures in organizations which have previously followed a more traditional approach to product costing (Cooper and Kaplan, 1991b) has resulted in some radical changes in the pattern of product line costings. The following example is designed to illustrate the type of situation in which ABC can result in a substantial revision to product costs.

DISCUSSION

The use of an ABC approach results in product costs which reflect more closely the resource demands and consumption of the products. This is achieved by treating the various elements of overhead separately and taking account of how each is differently related to production. The cost drivers are not perfect measures of resource consumption, but do give a better indication of it than the single base of direct labour hours.

The resultant product costs show a marked reduction in that of the standard switch and a significant increase in that of the customized one. In effect the labour hours basis had fairly evenly averaged overhead across the two products, leading to a cross-subsidization of the customized product. The same effect would occur where products were of differing sizes (as measured by their direct labour input) but, in fact, made similar demands per unit on the overhead resources. Here a labour hour basis of overhead cost absorption would result in an overcosting of the larger product and a cross-subsidization of the smaller product. ABC provides more visibility on the composition of overhead cost. It also highlights in this case the heavier demands which each unit of the customized switch places on resources by requiring relatively more input from quality control, set-up, purchasing and order processing.

The basis of these demands, the cost driver, is identified and it can become a focus point for management control efforts. The movement in unit costs is very marked. The customized switch has changed from being 123 per cent of the cost of the standard switch to 348 per cent. This swing has occurred by the redistribution of the overhead cost element, which only totals 36 per cent of total cost in Etron Ltd. Although within this category only a small portion is (production) volume rather than (various) activity driven, the considerable potential for ABC to result in substantially revised product costs is demonstrated.

The impact of the new ABC costs on product pricing will be one interesting issue arising from these situations. While those involved in marketing the standard switch may be happy to maintain existing margins and thereby allow prices to fall considerably, the price rises for the customized switches may be

EXAMPLE 3.5

Data:

Etron Ltd manufactures electronic switches. Two classes of switch are produced: the first is a standard design supplied to one large customer; the second involves the production of customized batches of the switch, each being modified slightly to suit the needs of individual customers. The following information has been gathered for the last year of operations.

1. *Production statistics*

	Total units produced	No. of production runs	No. of suppliers	No. of customer orders in period
Standard design	1 000 000	50	20	10
Customised designs	160 000	400	280	190

2. *Direct costs*

	Standard design £	Customized design* £
Direct materials	0.50	0.60
Direct labour (paid at a rate of £8.00 per hour)	0.40	0.50

*The extra direct costs represent the extra materials and labour required for customization.

3. *Indirect costs*

	£
Quality control (one inspection per production run)	90 000
Process set up (required for each production run)	135 000
Purchasing	105 000
Customer order processing	120 000
Occupancy costs (rent, heat, light, power, etc.)	150 000
	600 000

Continued

71

EXAMPLE 3.5
Continued

The cost drivers for these costs clearly include more than simply the number of labour hours worked. The demands placed on the activities are influenced respectively by the number of inspections, number of set-ups, number of suppliers, and number of orders. Perhaps only for occupancy cost are direct labour hours appropriate.

Etron have traditionally used a single direct labour hours basis for overhead absorption. The rate used during the year was £10.00 per direct labour hour, i.e. £600 000 of indirect costs ÷ 60 000 direct labour hours. The latter figure represents 1 million standard switches, each taking 1/20 hour and 160 000 customized switches, each taking 1/16 hour. The unit costs obtained by operation of the traditional costing system were as follows:

	Standard design £	Customized design £
Direct material	0.50	0.60
Direct labour	0.40	0.50
Overhead	0.50★	0.625★★
	1.40	1.725

★ 1/20 direct labour hour × £10

★★ 1/16 direct labour × £10

72

The adoption of an activity-based costing approach, in contrast, generates the following unit costs for Etron Ltd's products:

	Activity basis Standard design £	Customized design £
Direct material	0.50	0.60
Direct labour	0.40	0.50
Overheads	0.177★	2.644★★
	1.077	3.744
	£	£
★Quality control	0.011	0.500
Process set-up	0.015	0.750
Purchasing	0.021	0.525
Order processing	0.006	0.713
Occupancy	0.125	0.156
	0.177	2.644

Continued

EXAMPLE 3.5
Continued

Total costs

	Standard £		Customized £	
Quality control	10 000	(50 × £200)	80 000	(400 × £200)
Process set-up	15 000	(50 × £300)	120 000	(400 × £300)
Purchasing	21 000	(20 × £1050)	84 000	(80 × £1050)
Customer order processing	6 000	(10 × £600)	114 000	(190 × £600)
Occupancy	125 000	(50 000 × £2.50)	25 000	(10 000 × £2.50)
	177 000		423 000	

Unit costs	(÷ 1 000 000) 0.177	(÷ 160 000) 2.644

The above cost driver rates for each of the overhead activities have been derived as follows:

Quality control	= £ 90 000 ÷ 450 inspections	= £200 per inspection
Process set-up	= £135 000 ÷ 450 set ups	= £300 per set up
Purchasing	= £105 000 ÷ 100 suppliers	= £1 050 per supplier
Customer order processing	= £120 000 ÷ 200 customers	= £600 per customer order
Occupancy	= £150 000 ÷ 60 000 DLH	= £2.5 per DLH

considerable if the same policy is pursued, and as a lack of competitiveness may result, the continued existence of these product lines is called into question. The appropriateness of ABC unit cost information for this type of decision is discussed further in the following chapter.

ABC AND SERVICE COSTING

Service industries differ from the manufacturing sector in that they do not have a tangible physical output to use as a central cost object. However, as in manufacturing, service organizations acquire resources to permit the performance of activities which will result in the provision of a service to customers. Thus ABC provides an excellent basis for costing systems which will reflect how acquired resources have been consumed in order to generate the end result services. This suitability is reflected in its adoption within the banking, insurance, transport, education and health sectors.

In the service context, ABC involves establishing the framework of activities which comprise the organization. As Figure 3.4 shows, activities should be characterized in respect of how their outputs are utilized. Some exist merely to service other activities

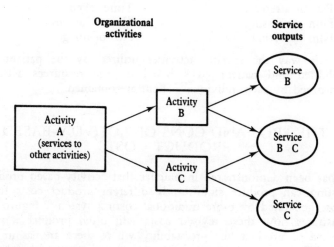

FIGURE 3.4 Service sector activity framework.

75

(A), while others contribute directly to the final services which are provided externally (B and C). This framework, coupled with an identification of cost drivers to facilitate the movement of costs, will ultimately allow costs to be attached in an appropriate manner to the final services.

In practice, ABC has resulted in a refinement of the costing practices adopted in the service sector. For example, in hospitals ABC has been used to refine the traditional daily rate for care and accommodation (Rotch, 1990) which was essentially a patient average cost, to one which distinguishes separate aspects of the services given to a patient. Accommodation costs are based on duration and location of stay. Nursing activity costs are attached to patients on the basis of time and the acuity level of the treatment required. Costs of other clinical services can also be attached to patients using specific cost drivers. One London hospital (Kirton, 1992) has applied ABC to its radiological services through use of the following cost pools and drivers:

Activities	*Cost driver* *(basis of cost charge to patients)*
Patient movement	No. of in-patients
Booking appointments	No. of patients
Patient reception	No. of patients
X-ray equipment preparation	Time taken
X-ray patient preparation	Time taken
Radiological examination	Time taken
Patient aftercare	Time taken
Film processing	No. of images
Film reporting	No. of images

In this way the specific activities utilized by the patient are identified and patient costs based on the resources actually consumed by each individual patient are obtained.

THE PROS AND CONS OF ACTIVITY-BASED PRODUCT COSTS

It has been demonstrated in practice that activity-based product costing can produce significantly different product costs from those generated by more traditional costing systems. Figure 3.5 illustrates how these revised costs will often produce a new pattern of product line profitability where there are, as in the earlier example, a variety of customized and standard products.

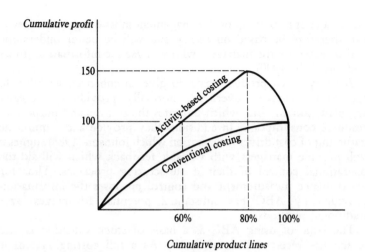

FIGURE 3.5 Profit line profitability profile.

ABC will highlight the drain on profitability caused by the customized products which have been subsidized by the standard products through the conventional costing system. Twenty per cent of products are shown to be loss-making with ABC, as profits peak with only 80 per cent of existing product lines, and indeed current profit levels could be achieved with only 60 per cent of existing products. Advocates of ABC would argue that its product costs more accurately reflect how resources have been consumed by each product line. Where convenient and general approaches have been used to cope with heterogeneous overhead costs, this is a difficult claim to refute, although in any complex production or service undertaking it is impossible to devise a system which will produce wholly accurate output costs. To claim perfection for ABC would thus clearly be wrong. However, in the types of situation described earlier in this chapter, ABC does appear to offer the best available approach to full absorption costing.

It is an approach to costing which is based upon a detailed knowledge of the overhead area of the business. An appreciation of what actually happens in the organization has to precede the selection of an appropriate set of activity cost pools and cost drivers. The system has to be based on this type of specific and detailed study if it is to be meaningful. Achieving this has the advantage of involving local management in its design. The results can therefore be based on reality and will be better understood and accepted by the managers who will use the information (Innes and Mitchell, 1990).

Activity-based product costs do give an enhanced visibility to the components of overhead, normally providing a greater segmentation and one which indicates the sources and purpose of resource consumption. In addition, they provide and require the gathering of cost driver information which Johnson (1988) suggests will provide managers with valuable feedback which will aid the operational control of their manufacturing processes. Thus for performance measurement and control purposes the information provided by ABC has substantial potential advantages over traditional methods.

The issue of using ABC as a basis of stock valuation is one which has received little attention. As a full costing system it will, in principle, meet the requirements of SSAP 9 and, given its ability to refine unitization in the overhead area, there should be little doubt about its ability to meet the "true and fair view" test of the auditor.

Within the realm of decision making, Johnson and Kaplan (1987b) have stressed the value of long-run product cost information as an input at a strategic level. They have also supported activity-based costing as providing the best indication of these costs. Over a medium to long-term time-span, all costs can vary. This is done by taking decisions which will alter the resources held and/or acquired, as well as those which will change the pattern of consumption (e.g. product-mix decisions) of the resources already at the firm's disposal.

ABC gives an indication of the way in which each product consumes resources, including the types of resource which may be influenced in the longer run. It therefore provides a basis (when compared with sales price) for directing management's attention to a strategic consideration of changes in the composition of the product portfolio (Cooper and Kaplan, 1991b). Indeed Shank (1990) casts doubt on the use of the alternative approach of using the contribution margin (sales less *only* variable costs) to make such decisions:

> The contribution margin mentality will lead you to keep everything.
> It will lead you to add products, it will lead you to never drop anything, it will lead you to always make instead of buy.

In any decision situation involving the alteration of product range mix or volume, a financial evaluation of the decision should properly involve an identification of how the future cash flows of the organization will be affected by the decision. Product cost information provides only a limited indication of this. Shank (1990) has shown concern that variable costs exclude many of the potential factors influencing future cash flows. Others have argued that ABC systems will produce costs which include factors which will not change in response to decisions (Sharp and Christensen, 1991). Activity-based product costs include information on many of the factors of concern to Shank (e.g. quality control, set-ups, etc.) but their reliability as bases for measurement of the real economic effect of the decisions is open to question. If the activity-based costs are historic then they, at best, provide only a basis for estimating future costs over a medium/long time period involving possibly organizational and technological changes.

When unitized, the activity pool costs may contain temporal cost allocations representing sunk historic costs such as depreciation and apportionments of resources which are common to several activities. Moreover, even when directly attributable to an activity, costs may be associated with providing the capacity for an activity to exist and will therefore be unaltered by the levels of cost driver variation stemming from changes in the production of one product from an extensive range (Roth and Borthwick, 1991). Alteration of activity resources may also actually create costs such as labour redundancy payments which the product costing system would not reflect.

Another difficulty occurs where cost drivers have a jointness which limits their value. For example, a purchase order may relate to more than one product line. How therefore should its cost be shared among them? Homogeneity of costs in each activity pool will also be limited and the availability of cost drivers which explain cost variation in a linear fashion is also doubtful.

Thus for decision making, neither ABC nor variable costing is perfect, but both may have a role to play (Koehler, 1991), particularly if differing decision time horizons are to be considered. Ultimately, however, it will be a matter of empirical observation, in organizations, as to which gives the better attention-directing signals to management about the components of their product range.

The susceptibility of a firm's situation to ABC providing improvements to unit cost information will be a key determinant in any assessment of the approach's worth. It should be remembered that the technical problems of jointness of costs and drivers are certainly not resolved by ABC, and the establishment of a system is frequently viewed as costly and time-consuming (Cobb *et al.*,

1992). However, the advantages outlined above may be of considerable import in situations where a longer-run perspective is necessary for the decision maker. A situational assessment should therefore underlie any decision of the value and suitability of ABC.

DISCUSSION TOPICS

1. Given below is the formal organization chart of Zirco Ltd, a manufacturer of remote control switches.

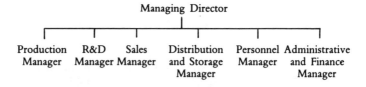

In which of the above areas of managerial responsibility would you expect to find the consumption of resource in respect of the following activities?
— quality control
— maintenance;
— customer order processing;
— resource procurement.
Discuss the significance of your findings for the design and operation of a costing system.

2. Outline the criteria you would set for the selection of a cost driver for any given activity cost pool.

3. Advocates of activity-based product costing suggest that it rectifies systematic costing errors caused by the use of convenient bases such as direct labour hours. Define three situations where such a situation might arise.

4. In what type of organization do you think the costs of an ABC system would outweigh its benefits?

5. Given the impossibility of ever identifying the precise product or service cost in a complex organization, do you think it is ever worthwhile to invest in a system which attempts the impossible?

4

Activity-Based Cost Management

INTRODUCTION

In their pursuit of customer satisfaction, management must ensure that the product or service output of their firm meets the demands of the market. To achieve this they should consider their organization's ability to deliver appropriate products and services, at the time when they are wanted, of a standard and quality that is expected, and at a price which is competitive. These objectives require balancing, as there are distinct trade-offs among them. Underlying them all, however, is the question of their cost. Strategies, policies and actions in respect of these factors will need to take account of the cost implications and indeed may involve establishing new cost requirements for various aspects of the business. These are the basic ingredients of cost management. To be effective, cost management must be based on a sound knowledge of the organization's cost structure and an appreciation of how costs are determined and therefore how they may be influenced. This understanding assists managers in exerting effective control over costs in pursuing their objectives. However, knowledge requires information. This chapter examines how the activity-based costing approach can contribute to just such an understanding.

The emergence of ABC in the mid-1980s was primarily directed at the generation of improved full product cost information which could be used to assess product line profitability. However, a wider potential for the measurement and analysis of cost in this way soon became apparent. ABC provided new insights into the factors which caused overhead cost. This provided the potential to aid managerial understanding of cost behaviour and contribute to more effective overhead cost measurement analysis and control. This chapter explores the various ways in which the activity-based approach has been incorporated into the cost management effort.

ACTIVITY COST VISIBILITY

Knowledge precedes understanding and ABC has contributed to management's knowledge of overhead costs in a way which enhances understanding by segmenting them on the basis of the processes (activities) which consume resources. It therefore shows management the reasons for acquiring and consuming resource, as for each activity the input/process/output situation is given the sort of visibility illustrated for purchasing in Figure 4.1.

This type of analysis helps managers to identify more fully the value chain of activities undertaken within their organization (Shank and Govindarajan, 1992). Within the overhead area it allows managers to see what they are spending (in terms of resource type), where they are utilizing these acquired resources (in terms of activities) and what they are getting for their money (in terms of the output measure or cost driver). Costs and benefits are linked together, frequently for the first time, in a way which management can use to assess performance. The cost driver rate,

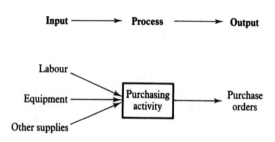

FIGURE 4.1 Purchasing activity analysis.

for example, can be viewed as the unit cost of an activity's output and, as such, will given one indication of the productivity and efficiency of the work being done. Moreover, the existence of output measures provides a basis for incorporating the basic ideas of total quality management in the overhead area (Steiner, 1990). The accuracy of purchase ordering can be monitored with delays, lead times and errors of different types reported. This can be part of an effort to eliminate problems and improve service to the activity's customers, so that ultimately the business will run more smoothly and efficiently.

The application of the ABC approach normally provides a novel perspective on the organization's costs. Activities frequently do not mirror the formal organization structure (see Figure 4.2) and data on their costs has therefore to be retrieved from several distinct formal segments of the firm.

This can be a source of difficulty in implementing and using ABC, as responsibility for both an activity and its costs can be unclear where departmental boundaries are crossed (Innes and Mitchell, 1991b) and some organizations have had to restructure to cope with this problem. In these situations, however, the resultant information does normally provide a new input to the monitoring and assessment of cost. Indeed it is this contribution, rather than its use in product costing, that may well be deemed its most valuable aspect (Innes and Mitchell, 1991b) and of sufficient merit on its own right to justify the establishment of an ABC system.

This type of ABC information may prove useful on two levels. First, within each activity, the analysis can extend to sub-activities or even actions or tasks and the flow, timing and cost of these

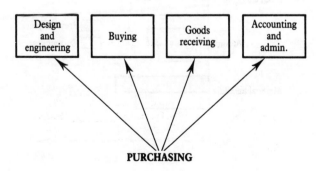

FIGURE 4.2 The location of purchasing activity.

recorded. Mapping and annotating these for each activity in a systems format (Morrow and Hazell, 1992) can provide a convenient presentation for this type of analysis. Examples of staff and time savings have been dramatic, when activities have first been given this enhanced visibility (Innes and Mitchell, 1990). Second, the analysis can be based on a listing and cost comparison among the activities selected for the ABC system. This provides a profile of the activity costs of the organization (see Figure 4.3), one which will give an awareness of the pattern of resource consumption, as well as permitting assessment of trends over time and intra-organizational comparisons in multi-plant firms.

Both of these novel types of analysis may be enhanced by screening the identified activities in terms of their worth to the organization. Most commonly the attribute "value added" has been used as a basis for this. Activities which do not "add value" to the product supplied to the customer become targets for cost reduction (Berliner and Brimson, 1989). Judgement must be exercised in classifying activities in this way and in using the resultant analysis, as many activities may appear non-value added but at least in the short run may be essential to the smooth operation of the business. Thus, as Table 4.1 shows, a whole range of activities and sub-activities are exposed as areas where the elimination of cost becomes a priority. Many of the non-

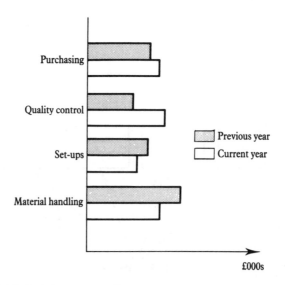

FIGURE 4.3 Activity cost profile.

Table 4.1 Value added v. non-value added activities.

Activity	Value added	Non-value added
Purchasing:		
Vetting suppliers	X	
Producing orders	X	
Returning goods		X
Correcting orders		X
Customer order processing:		
Assessing credit rating		X
Liaising with customer	X	
Expediting delivery		X
Dealing with returns inwards		X
Quality control:		
Supplies received		X
In process		X
On completion		X
Material scheduling:		
Identifying line needs	X	
Storage		X
Movement store to line		X

value added activities identified here are concerned with coping with deficiencies of the system, and their exposure highlights the need for things to be "done right first time" and can indicate programmes to help achieve this. Care has also to be taken that the organization can function effectively without those activities which are removed.

One interesting variation on this theme has been proposed by Bellis-Jones and Hand (1989). They argue that the components of identified activities should be analysed into three categories: core, support and diversionary. For sales activity the time spent in contact with customers and potential customers might be deemed core work, while travelling time would be support activity and dealing with sales order processing errors would be diversionary. Indeed, according to Bellis-Jones and Hand, the latter two classes often account for the major portion of activities. Their identification and costing emphasizes the need to cut down on the resource not attributed to core work. Thus a regional location or improved communication system might be considered to reduce travel time, while a simplification of order filling procedures and the institution of a total quality philosophy could be a response to the diversionary problem of order errors. However, care has always to be taken that the extra costs of these initiatives do not outweigh their benefits and the resultant activity cost savings. It is also possible to link cost reductions with the level of service provided by activities. A range of alternative service levels and their respective costs can be generated to give management a series of options on how costs might be reduced and what the implications of each would be for the operation of the organization.

COST BEHAVIOUR PATTERNS

The accounting literature takes a rather myopic view of how costs behave. Generally their behaviour is analysed and measured in respect of only one driving force – production volume. Moreover although most texts give some recognition to the possible different patterns of how costs behave as volume changes, the simplifying and convenient two-way split into the fixed cost category (where costs do not change as volume varies) and variable cost category (where costs vary linearly with volume) is then made and used as a basis for contribution measurement and decision analyses involving product range, mix and output.

The categorization of a major component of cost as fixed or unchanging has been condemned by Kaplan (1988) for the neglect which it has engendered among accountants. Furthermore, in reality the overhead costs classified as fixed certainly do not exhibit a no-change pattern over time. In many organizations it is these costs which have exhibited some of the highest growth rates (Miller and Vollman, 1985). Clearly more resource is being acquired and used in these areas. If volume increases are not the cause of this growth the management accountant should discover, analyse and report on what factors are driving it. Only when this type of information is available can management accounting contribute to effective cost management in the area.

Many of the costs susceptible to an activity-based analysis fell into the fixed cost category. ABC provided an initial indication that these costs were primarily influenced by the volumes of each activity's throughput, rather than by the volume of production output. Thus the availability of cost driver information provided a set of factors which could be used to explain "fixed" cost behaviour. In turn, this required some assumption to be made as to the nature of the relationship between cost drivers and cost. For activity-based product costing a linear relationship was implicitly assumed (Noreen, 1991). The realism of this assumption depends upon there being only insignificant activity costs fixed in relation to the selected cost driver, a characteristic claimed by Cooper (1989) and a constant cost driver unit variable cost (no economies or diseconomies from altering cost driver volume). However, the generation over time of this data through the operation of the ABC system will provide a basis for the derivation of more realistic activity cost behaviour patterns, should this be deemed necessary.

Another application of activity-based product costing data in this area has been idea of structuring overhead cost in a way which highlights the different levels at which it is incurred (Cooper and Kaplan, 1991b). A five-layer structure may be used to group the various cost driver rates (see Table 4.2).

Table 4.2 The ABC cost hierarchy.

Level 1	Unit basis	Costs are primarily dependent on the volume of production. This category will therefore include costs such as machine power.
Level 2	Batch basis	Costs are primarily dependent on the number of batches. This category will include the costs of set-up and batch monitoring.
Level 3	Process level	Costs are primarily dependent on the existence of a process. This category will include such costs as quality control and supervision.
Level 4	Product level	Costs are primarily dependent on the existence of a product group or line. This category will include such costs as product management and parts administration.
Level 5	Facility level	Costs are primarily dependent on the existence of a production facility or plant. This category will include such costs as rent and rates and general management.

This analysis of cost highlights the decision level at which each element of cost can be influenced. For example, the reduction of production cost levels will not simply depend on a general reduction in output volumes, but also on reorganizing production to perhaps increase batch size and reduce batch volume, on eliminating or modifying a process, on cutting out or merging product lines or on altering or removing facility capacity. If unit product cost information is presented in this way, managers are alerted to the whole range of factors which can have an impact on cost. All of the non-unit level costs contain an element of allocation when reported in unit terms, and this characteristic is highlighted under the ABC approach to the decision possibilities for altering costs. Traditional product costs do not reveal this and consequently may give the misleading impression that the cost object (the unit of output) drives the full cost.

Through disclosures of this type, ABC helps managers understand costs and therefore contributes to their effective management. It provides an attention-directing signal to management, based upon a comparison of the cost of resources consumed by a product in order to return a given market price. This signal targets particular products for the initiation of exercises to determine the future financial implications of expanding or reducing volumes, improving efficiency or changing the product design. ABC triggers these assessments and does not provide an instant answer for them, although it can, through the above cost hierarchy, provide a more realistic basis for modelling costs and undertaking "what if" analyses than is possible with the traditional fixed/variable cost split.

CUSTOMER PROFITABILITY ANALYSIS

The ABC concept has also been used to provide a focus on the profitability of the trading relationship between an organization and each of its customers (Bellis-Jones, 1989; O'Guin and Rebischke, 1992). This is achieved by an identification of the costs which are driven by the customer and which can therefore lead to significantly different profits from the sale of the same basic product to different customers. In effect the customer, rather than the product, becomes the cost object. Table 4.3 lists some of the major types of factor which can cause customer costs to differ.

The ABC approach provides a methodology for attributing costs such as these in a meaningful way to the sales transactions

Table 4.3 Customer-driven costs.

• Supply and delivery patterns	Influenced by the frequency of delivery, e.g. a JIT user customer will require a more costly delivery service than one which maintains a large buffer stock.
• Customer location	Distribution costs, communication and contact costs are all influenced by distance.
• Quality provided	Different customers may require different standards – again a JIT user will normally need a high-quality supply to function effectively.
• Provision of after-sales service	The terms may be negotiated individually with customers.
• Required documentation	This is determined by the needs of the customer.
• Sales and promotion effort	This may be geared to different groups of customers, who may be attracted by different attributes of the product/service being offered.
• Discounts given	Repeat business, special relationships, offers or promptness of paying can all differ among customers.

with customers, a basic component element of aggregate profit. This is achieved by a procedure akin to that applied to product costing. First, the activities stemming from factors such as those listed in Table 4.3 are identified and costed. Second, a cost driver is identified either for these activities or for segments of them. Segmentation may be required to enhance cost homogeneity and ensure the appropriateness of the driver selected. The period activity cost divided by the period cost driver volume provides a rate which can then be used to cost the activity consumption by each customer. In order to do this, a record has to be kept of the cost driver volumes attributable to each customer.

Example 4.1 shows how the ABC approach can generate substantially different costs and customer-derived profit in a situation where each of three customers buys exactly the same volume of the same product.

EXAMPLE 4.1

Customer profitability measurement, ABC v. traditional approach

Data

1. Product X (sold to 3 customers):
   Unit production cost £40.00
   Unit selling price £75.00

2. Sales:
   Customer A – sales of 10000 units per annum
   Customer B – sales of 10000 units per annum
   Customer C – sales of 10000 units per annum

3. Other non-production overhead costs:

	£
Delivery	220000
Quality inspection	200000
Salesmen	80000
After sales service	100000
	600000

Continued

4. Period activity volumes:

	Customer A	Customer B	Customer C
No. of deliveries	2 500 (10 per working day)	50 (1 per week)	12 (1 per month)
No. of inspections	10 000 (each unit)	500 (10 from each delivery)	0 (none)
No. of salesmen visits	200	24	6
After sales visits	200	100	50

Customer profitability

1. Traditional (apportioning non-production costs on the basis of production cost):

Overhead rate $= \dfrac{£600\,000}{£1\,200\,000} = £0.50$ per £ of production cost

	Unit cost*	Unit selling price	Unit profit	Total profit
Customer A	60.00	75.00	15.00	150 000
Customer B	60.00	75.00	15.00	150 000
Customer C	60.00	75.00	15.00	150 000
				450 000

*£40 production cost plus £20 non-production cost.

91

EXAMPLE 4.1
Continued

2. ABC:

Cost driver rates

– Delivery	$\dfrac{(£220\,000)}{2\,562}$	= £85.87 per delivery
– Inspections	$\dfrac{(£200\,000)}{10\,500}$	= £19.04 per inspection
– Salesmen	$\dfrac{(£80\,000)}{230}$	= £347.83 per salesman visit
– After sales	$\dfrac{(£100\,000)}{350}$	= £285.71 per after sales visit

	Production cost £	Non-production cost** £	Total cost £	Unit cost £	Unit selling price £	Unit profit/ (loss) £	Total profit/ (loss) £
Customer A	400 000	531 783	931 783	93.18	75.00	(18.18)	(181 800)
Customer B	400 000	50 813	450 813	45.08	75.00	29.92	299 200
Customer C	400 000	17 404	417 404	41.74	75.00	33.26	332 600
							450 000

		Customer A £	Customer B £	Customer C £
Delivery**	2500 deliveries @ £85.87	214 675		
	50 deliveries @ £85.87		4294	
	12 deliveries @ £85.87			1031
Inspection	100 000 inspections @ £19.04	190 400		
	500 inspections @ £19.04		9600	
Salesmen visits	200 visits @ £347.83	69 566		
	24 visits @ £347.83		8347	
	6 visits @ £347.83			2087
After sales visits	200 visits @ £285.71	57 142		
	100 visits @ £285.71		28 572	
	50 visits @ £285.71			14 286
		531 783	50 813	17 404

DISCUSSION

The ABC approach reflects the consumption of resource by each customer, and in Example 4.1 customer A clearly makes by far the heaviest demands on on-production resource, consequently showing a substantial unit loss in its trading relationship with the organization. Both customers B and C show higher profits. In effect the traditional costing basis has resulted in a marked cross-subsidization of A by B and C. Thus the ABC analysis provides an attention-directing signal to management, one which should raise the following issues for consideration:

- Should we continue a trading relationship with customers like A? (NB The ABC loss is not a definitive guide to answering this question, as not all of the customer-driven costs may be avoided if the customer is dropped.)
- Can we cut the consumption of resources involved in servicing customers like A? (And to what extent can we turn these cuts into future cash outflow reductions?)
- Can we increase the price charged to customers like A?
- Should we pursue policies to foster customers of the B and C type?

Example 4.1 shows that customers generating the same product volume of business can actually contribute very differently to profitability. Other studies of this type (Kaplan, 1991) have also shown that the analysis of profitability over all customers can be insightful, with the smaller volume, service-demanding customers often showing net losses in their trading relationship. The pattern is shown in Figure 4.4, where 20 per cent of customers generate 100 per cent of profits, 50 per cent provide a higher total profit, and the final 50 per cent actually do not cover full cost. Again similar questions to those listed above should be considered by management. This type of information can therefore initiate and contribute to strategy formulation by providing a basis for targeting promotional efforts and for eliminating or redirecting resource use in the non-production sector.

PERFORMANCE MEASUREMENT

As activities can consume so many of the resources utilized by an organization, the measurement of performance at an activity level will be of particular value to management. Through

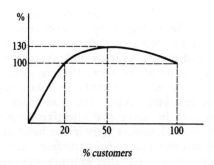

FIGURE 4.4 Customer profitability analysis.

performance measurement, improvement can be monitored, problems exposed, their causes identified, and behaviour influenced, hopefully in a positive way. Johnson (1988) suggests that the non-financial cost driver measures used in an ABC system can frequently provide a means of achieving all of these benefits.

At the level of operational control of the production process and its support areas, cost driver data impinge directly on the activities to be managed. Whereas costs are of themselves too abstract to "manage", variables such as set-up times, number of inspections and number of purchase orders are more easily understood and influenced directly by those supervising the related activities. For example, set-up times can be reduced by revising work procedures, inspections eliminated by "getting it right" first time and the complexity of purchase ordering reduced by simplification. Johnson's (1988) view is that a non-financial performance measurement system of this type is an essential ingredient of the information system for any organization whose ambition is to become or remain a world-class manufacturer.

However, ABC also provides financial performance measurement through both the activity costs and the cost driver rates which it generates. Where the rates are based on activity output volumes, then they will provide an indication of the productivity and cost efficiency of the activity. Their existence should therefore enhance the cost consciousness of management associated with the activity. Moreover, the motivational effect of this aspect of ABC can be powerful (Cooper and Turney, 1990), as management strive to improve performance as reflected in the measure. This is particularly true in respect of product design, a stage in the product life cycle where a high proportion of costs are committed.

Providing designers with cost driver rate information which indicates the cost of the transactions underlying overhead contributes to their ability to design cost effective products (Dolinsky and Vollman, 1991). In one celebrated case Tektronix, an American electronics firm, devised its ABC system in order to influence its product designers to be more cost effective (Jonez and Wright, 1987). The Tektronix designers were in the habit of building new products which incorporated novel parts from new suppliers, but in many instances it was felt that existing standard parts could equally well have been used. This behaviour led to a proliferation in their supplier numbers, the number of parts handled by the firm and in their inspection and ordering activities. Consequently direct material-related overheads were growing at a rate which gave cause for concern. The accountants who had previously attached overhead to products on a direct labour hours basis therefore devised an overhead absorption method of the ABC type which better reflected the pattern of cost incurrence and which penalized the product designers for use of new non-standard parts. Example 4.2 outlines the procedure adopted.

EXAMPLE 4.2

The Tektronix ABC system

Data

Material procurement overhead for period = £10 million
Number of different parts utilized in period = 10 000 parts

Overhead absorption

1. Rate per part number = £1 000 (£10 million ÷ 10 000 parts)

2. Low usage part – say 100 per annum
   High usage part – say 40 000 per annum

3. Overhead cost per low usage part = £10 (£1 000 ÷ 100 parts)
   Overhead cost per high usage part = £0.25 (£1 000 ÷ 40 000 parts)

Procurement overhead was driven predominantly by the number of parts actively in use. The new system utilized this cost driver in a meaningful way.

Where a high usage item (i.e. an established and standard part from an already accredited supplier) was used, it attracted an overhead burden of only £0.25. This is only one-fortieth of the cost of a completely new part, which would not be bought at anything like the same volume. Designers working to cost targets were therefore motivated to utilize standard high usage parts where possible.

The adage, "you get what you measure", emphasizes the motivational strength of performance measurement. Given this potential, it is essential that measures selected do influence people to behave in a manner congruent with the organization's aims. This is a notoriously difficult objective in itself, as consequences may often be unforeseen, e.g. Tektronix designers might have been led to produce fewer innovative products, as a result of the new costing system. Furthermore, human ingenuity often leads to manipulation of performance measures. The cost driver rate used in an ABC system can be improved (i.e. reduced) in two ways. First the numerator (the cost incurred) can be reduced. Second the denominator (the cost driver variable) can be increased. Provided this increase is accompanied by a less than proportionate increase in the numerator (i.e. there is an element of the activity cost fixed with respect to the cost driver), then the rate will improve even though the total cost has risen. Where the cost driver rate is used as a performance measure, staff may therefore be motivated to increase the number of set-ups, inspections, etc. Without care, the system can become dysfunctional and self-defeating.

BUDGETING AND CONTROL

Due to the enhanced visibility which it gives to overhead costing and its use of cost drivers which indicate levels of activity workload, ABC can provide a valuable basis for establishing and using budgets in the overhead area (Brimson and Fraser, 1991). An analysis of activities, their previous and current costs and the throughput levels at which they have operated, gives a sound foundation for estimating and planning future spend. Activities can be examined individually and a justification required not simply for their existence but also for their organization and the level of service which is involved. Activity "customers" can even

EXAMPLE 4.3

Budget reports and ABC

	Original budget		Actual			Variance
	Cost driver	£000s	Cost driver	£000s		£000s
Inspection*	1 000 inspections	140	1 100	165	inspections	25 U
Set-up	100 set-ups	400	80	410	set-ups	10 U
Purchasing	2 000 orders	50	2 200	55	orders	5 U
Material handling	800 movements	200	1 000	290	movements	90 U
		790		920		130 U

*An example of possible further analysis:

1. *Capacity*

		Comment
Budgeted capacity	1 000 inspections	Why was activity level higher than expected?
Capacity provided by actual cost (£165 000 ÷ £140)	1 179 inspections	Why was capacity provision greater than use?
Actual capacity used	1 100 inspections	Can spare capacity be identified and cut?

2. *Variances*

Budget 1,000 inspections @ £140 = £140 000	£14 000 U	Activity exceeds expectation (see above comments)
Flexed budget 1 100 inspections @ £140 = £154 000	£11 000 U	Spending exceeds expectation (consider cost control in quality area)
Actual 1 100 inspections @ £150 = £165 000		

become involved in the process in order to assist in judging the resource needs and benefits of activities. Cost driver data can help to identify the expected costs to compare with benefits in arriving at decisions on this latter issue. Thus ABC can facilitate the budgeting process in all of the following ways:

- Identification of the activities to which resources may be committed.
- Examination of the value of activities to the organizational objectives, leading to a prioritization ranking for scarce resource provision during the budgeting process.
- Assessment of the possible levels of service required from these activities, including the zero option.
- A meaningful match between areas of responsibility or "ownership" and costs.
- Estimation of the cost implications of alterations to activities (either their organization or workload levels) which will enable cost/benefit analyses to be made.

While the process of establishing the budget is enhanced by ABC in all of these ways, there are also potential benefits to be gained in terms of the budget/actual performance reports generated by the accounting system. Simply, the extended variety of cost pools will provide a new perspective on the source of cost variances. Furthermore, the cost driver data will provide another ingredient which will assist in giving management an indication of activity volumes, capacity, capacity usage and efficiency. Example 4.3 demonstrates the type of report which can be produced where ABC is in use.

This activity-based budget report directs attention at the use of resource in the overhead area. It shows where spend has exceeded the budget and where that excess may be mitigated, at least in part, by higher than expected workloads (cost driver levels). It highlights areas for investigation, but does not explain why cost driver volumes are different from budget. In addition, cost driver data gives an indication of the capacities expected, provided and used for each activity. It therefore profiles the activities upon which the system is based in terms of their capacity usage. Where there is a constant overprovision, a signal is given to management to consider the possibility of initiating some cost reduction action.

CONCLUSION

The potential of an activity-based approach to aid cost management is illustrated in the novelty and variety of the types of information reviewed in this chapter. All of them have the capacity to direct management's attention to areas where action can improve profitability. While further study of the financial implications of that action may well be required before decisions are made, the significance of ABC is that it does help to identify the opportunities and problems which should be the concern of managers.

DISCUSSION TOPICS

1. "Our position remains that ABC is logically flawed and the case for its application is both questionable and unproven" (Piper and Walley, 1990).

   Do you consider that the debate between Robin Cooper and John Piper and Walley was won, drawn or lost?

   Useful references:
   Cooper, R. (1990), "Explicating the Logic of ABC", *Management Accounting (UK)*, November, pp. 58–60.
   Piper, J. and Walley, P. (1990), "Testing ABC Logic", *Management Accounting (UK)*, September, pp. 37, 42.
   Piper, J. and Walley, P. (1991), "ABC Relevence Not Found", *Management Accounting (UK)*, March, pp. 42, 54.

2. What are the major advantages of knowing the cost of the main activities of an organization?

3. How detailed does activity analysis have to be in order to permit a meaningful core/support diversionary analysis? Give examples to illustrate your answer. (Hint: distinguishing the terms action, task, activity and process may help.)

4. The following activity listing is from the Die Pressing Process involved in motor car manufacture. Which do you consider to be value adding?

Activity	Category	
	Value adding	Non-value adding
Off-loading of material to storage		
Identification tagging of material		
Material quality checking		
Booking material into stock		
Move material to production facility		
Load material into feeder		
Prepare and locate die		
Synchronize die and material on press		
Run trials		
Check trials		
Make necessary adjustments		

| *Activity* | *Category* | |
| | *Value adding* | *Non-value adding* |

Run production
Run quality checks
Move material to press
Load output
Book output into work in process
Move output to storage
Remove die

5. "Activity-based costing facilitates the use of a zero based or priority based approach to budgeting". Explain how ABC can fulfil this role.
6. The choice of cost drivers will have a considerable impact on behaviour within the organization. Discuss.
7. The customer is a more important cost object than the product or service. Discuss.

5

Overhead Cost Analysis and Management: Other Approaches

INTRODUCTION

This chapter reviews a range of approaches which have been developed to provide information that will assist in the management of overhead cost. They provide alternatives to the activity-based approaches discussed in the preceding chapter, but are not mutually exclusive and in some instances complement and build on the ABC approach. They therefore represent additional components of the accountant's "tool kit" for addressing the problems of analysing and controlling overheads.

The first part of this chapter examines approaches which can be applied generally within the overhead cost area. These are followed by an examination of some examples of specific types of overhead cost, showing how the more general approaches can be tailored to suit particular classes of overhead.

GENERAL APPROACHES

Budgeting

It is a traditional tenet of accounting control that actual performance should be reviewed against the benchmark of an *ex ante* budget or budget-derived standard, based on managerial objectives and plans. The variances from this comparison then provide the feedback necessary for management to assess the realism of their initial expectations and the progress being made towards the achievement of their aims. The segmentation of variances further helps to pinpoint areas to which management's attention should be particularly directed. The process can therefore support the linking of responsibilities to performance and facilitate a management-by-exception approach to the running of an organization.

Normal practice in establishing a budget is to begin with an estimate of future sales volumes and revenues and to derive from this an estimate of the resources required (and hence the costs involved) to achieve it. In the specific area of overhead costs, a number of elements may be involved in determining the budget.

The previous year's situation will often provide a starting point for the exercise, as it gives an indication of existing resources employed within the organization. Indeed the practice of simply adding an inflation allowance forecast to previous year figures to derive an overhead budget is perhaps the simplest, quickest and most convenient way of creating a budget. However, it will not necessarily motivate employees to be cost-conscious or to produce the best feedback information for management, as it incorporates all of the existing inefficiencies and slack of the business and takes no account of changes in many of the other factors determining cost levels within an organization, e.g. adoption of new technologies, improvements in training and the alteration of product volumes, mix and range. Furthermore, managerial strategy may require movements in overhead resource commitment, for example to improve product quality or delivery performance. In order to reflect these factors and produce a more useful budget, the setting process may be built up from a more fundamental analysis undertaken for each type of overhead cost within each overhead department. These will reflect not only the starting position of these departments but also the likely circumstances and utilization of the departments for the forthcoming period and will be based on an awareness of the expected sales and production activity which they have to support.

These approaches, however, place considerable emphasis on the status quo, i.e. the nature of previous and existing resourcing of the overhead functions. As a means of questioning existing resourcing patterns it may be valuable to begin the budget-setting process from scratch, i.e. a zero base. On this basis departmental managers are required to justify *all* resources which are to be incorporated in their budget. The procedure is known as zero-based budgeting (see, for example, Stonich, 1976). It leads to a questioning of the need for current methods of operation and the consideration of alternative more cost-effective means of providing required services. For example, the buying-in of services such as security or transport will be compared with the cost of in-house provision. It requires a clear identification of the workload carried by each department and so it brings a greater visibility to the whole overhead area. To aid cost reduction it is usually combined with a prioritizing of the activities undertaken in each overhead department to reflect how critical they are to the functioning of that area of the business. Thus the costs and benefits of activities are highlighted and this gives management the opportunity to judge the trade-off between expenditure and benefits both within and among departments. The approach allows attacks to be made on budgetary slack and empire-building. It is therefore an effective way of achieving cost reduction, but it often involves substantial change within an organization and is therefore best handled in a participative manner, if behavioural problems are to be avoided.

Variance analysis

The comparison of budget or standard with actual performance generates the variance information which provides the main feedback to management on how well their plans are being met. If a system of fixed budgeting is in use then the *ex ante* budget is a fixed basis for comparison with the actual costs incurred. This can produce rather misleading variances where overheads which do vary with production volume are significant and the actual production volume achieved in the period differs substantially from that set in the budget. Thus, in Example 5.1 the favourable variance on power of £20 000 in the fixed budget analysis does not necessarily indicate sound cost control, as it was incurred during a period when production and therefore consumption of power was only 80 per cent of that expected when the original budget was set. The flexing of the budget to reflect this shows that only £200 000 (80 per cent of the original budget) should have been incurred in power costs, given the actual production achieved. Thus, in fact, an unfavourable variance of £30 000 exists on the power element of overhead.

This idea of flexing the budget is facilitated in practice by using standard costs. These are simply budgeted unit costs. The standard cost of power in Example 5.1 would be £2.50 derived from the

EXAMPLE 5.1
Fixed v. flexible budgets

1. Fixed budget analysis

Overhead	Category (F = Fixed) (V = Variable)	Original budget (based on production of 100 000 units) £'000s	Actual (based on production of 80 000 units) £'000s	Volume (F = Favourable) (A = Adverse) £'000s
Power	V	250	230	20F
Maintenance	V	150	120	30F
Quality control	V	100	150	50A
Rent	F	420	390	30F
Machine depreciation	F	430	350	80F
Insurance	F	150	110	40F

2. Flexible budget analysis

Overhead	Category (F = Fixed) (V = Variable)	Flexed budget (unit standard cost × actual production volume) £'000s	Actual (based on production of 8 000 units) £'000s	Volume (F = Favourable) (A = Adverse) £'000s
Power	V	200	230	30A
Maintenance	V	120	120	NIL
Quality control	V	80	150	70A
Rent	F	336★	340	4A
Machine depreciation	F	344★	350	6A
Insurance	F	120★	110	10F

★The flexing of fixed costs by volume is clearly a questionable practice. Its implications are discussed further below.

original budget (£250 000 ÷ 100 000). Applying this standard cost to the 80 000 units actually produced gives the flexed budget for power (80 000 units × £2.50 = £200 000).

Standard overhead production costs are usually expressed not by individual cost type such as power, maintenance or insurance but by the totals for the fixed and variable classes of overhead. As they will normally be attached to units by means of an overhead rate, the standard cost will show their computation in terms of the rate currently in use. Where working time is considered to be the main causal factor of variable overhead cost, a labour hour basis will be used and the unit cost would appear as follows:

$$
\begin{array}{lr}
 & £ \\
\text{Variable overhead} - \text{10 direct labour hours @ £0.50 =} & 5.00 \\
\text{Fixed overhead} - \text{10 direct labour hours @ £1.00 =} & 10.00 \\
\text{Standard overhead cost per unit} = & \overline{} \\
 & 15.00
\end{array}
$$

These overhead rates are based on the assumption that the 100 000 units were to take 1 000 000 direct labour hours in the original budget for this product, i.e. 10 direct labour hours are allowed for each unit. If it is ascertained that the 8000 units actually produced took 900 000 direct labour hours with the actual fixed overhead costs totalling £800 000 then the overhead cost variance can be further segmented as shown in Example 5.2.

This segmentation aims to link the variances more closely to their causes and to specific managerial responsibilities within the organization. For variable overhead cost it is based upon the two basic factors underlying cost, i.e. first the price paid to acquire resources, and second the efficiency with which the acquired resources are used. Thus the variable overhead costs actually incurred (£500 000) are compared with what should have been incurred for a working period of 900 000 hours, which was the actual time worked by the labour force (i.e. £450 000, the standard rate set for one working hour of £0.50 × 900 000 hours). The adverse variance of £50 000 is therefore due to a higher price being paid for overhead of actual resources during the period than had been expected when the standard was set. To investigate the causes of this, one would examine the components of overhead shown in Example 5.2 and look to factors affecting the spend of each, such as the type of power used (e.g. less cheap-rate electricity being utilized, or an unexpected rise in the general tariffs).

However, while 900 000 hours were actually worked and so required this level of variable overhead cost, the actual production level of 80 000 units should only have taken 800 000 hours, had employee performance been at standard. Thus inefficiency resulting in more work time and therefore more variable overhead gave rise to a further unfavourable adverse variance of £50 000 (100 000 hours at £0.50 per hour). The search for causes here will be directed at the reasons for the inefficiency which caused the extra labour hours to be worked (e.g. machine breakdowns or high staff turnover during the period).

The utility of this variance information on variable overheads is based on the validity of three assumptions:

1. That the unit standard is of reasonable accuracy. A variance can be due to the standard being too tight or too loose, rather than to the influence of operational factors. Regular assessment and revision of the standard is therefore necessary.

2. That the basis of the overhead rate (direct labour hours in the above case) provides a sound explanation of the variability of overhead cost. If this is not the case, and the development of ABC has shown the use of a single volume-related base such as labour hours will often be of dubious accuracy, then the use of a series of factors reflecting cost behaviour patterns may give a better indication of what should have been spent on variable overheads (Solomons, 1968). If, for example, power costs varied with machine hours, maintenance with number of breakdowns and quality control with the number of inspections, then a predetermined rate could be set for each and then applied to the actual levels of these factors in the relevant period to establish what spending should have been and so permit the computation of a more meaningful spending variance (see Example 5.3 below). This approach allows the variance to be segmented by type of cost to assist in the tracing of cause. Note that the revised spending variance is considerably less than that computed in the conventional fashion and that it is in the area of quality control cost that management attention should be directed for the cause.

3. That there is a linear relationship between cost and volume. This is implicit in the computation of both the standard variable and fixed overhead cost of actual production which is achieved simply by multiplying the unit standard cost by the actual number of units produced. Where the overheads are primarily influenced by volume, the figure for standard cost of producing may be meaningful, but where the

EXAMPLE 5.2
Overhead cost variances

Variable overhead variances

(1) Actual variable overhead cost of actual production	(2) Actual use of resource causing the variable overhead cost at the standard cost rate	(3) Standard variable overhead cost of actual production
	900 000 hours × £0.50	80 000 units × 10 hrs = 800 000 hrs × £0.50
= £500 000	= £450 000	= £400 000

Spending variance £50 000A

Efficiency variance £50 000A

Total variable overhead variance £100 000A

Fixed overhead variances

(1) Actual fixed overhead cost of actual production	(2) Original budget for fixed overhead	(3) Standard fixed overhead cost of actual production
	100 000 units × 10 hrs = 1 000 000 hrs × £1.00	80 000 units × 10 hrs = 800 000 hrs × £1.00
= £850 000	= £1 000 000	= £800 000

Spending
variance
£150 000F

Volume
variance
£200 000A

Total fixed
overhead variance

£50 000A

EXAMPLE 5.3

Variable overhead spending variance using multiple absorption bases

Original budget

	£	Causal factors		Pre-determined rate
				£
Power	250 000	Machine hours	(100 000)	£2.50/machine hour
Maintenance	150 000	No. of breakdowns	(500)	£300 per breakdown
Quality control	100 000	No. of inspections	(2 000)	£50 per inspection

Actual performance

Machine hours worked	95 000
Number of breakdowns	430
Number of inspections	2 200

Spending variance

	Actual spend £'000s	What should have been spend £'000s	Variance £'000s
Power	230	237.5 (95000 machine hrs × £2.50)	7.5F
Maintenance	120	129 (430 breakdowns × £300)	9.0F
Quality control	150	110 (2200 inspections × £50)	40.0A
			23.5A

relationship is either not strong or is non-linear, then it will not provide a good standard for comparison. Indeed where fixed overheads are concerned, the figure may be viewed as nonsensical because its computation is based on the assumption that overheads do vary with production volume. By definition, the exact opposite is true of fixed overheads. Figure 5.1 illustrates this problem clearly by showing how the standard fixed overhead cost of production line actually assumes the pattern that one would expect of variable overhead costs.

The conventional fixed overhead spending variance (actual v. original budget) represents a comparison which has some validity. However, for fixed overhead, the efficiency variance is normally replaced by a volume variance, as production efficiency is not a determinant of the level of fixed overhead. Instead a volume variance (original budget v. standard cost of actual production) is computed. This too has limitations, as it utilizes the rather meaningless standard fixed overhead cost figure. If favourable (unfavourable) the volume variance simply indicates that a higher (lower) volume than that budgeted was produced. This volume

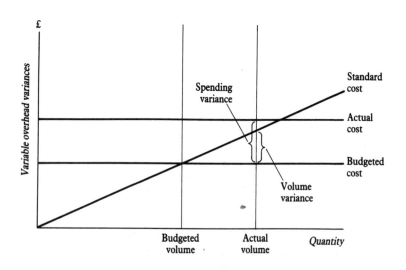

FIGURE 5.1 Fixed overhead cost variances.
Source: Based on Solomons, 1968.

114

difference is expressed in financial terms through multiplication by the standard fixed overhead rate. Horngren (1967) suggests that this variance is in fact more meaningfully expressed in physical terms (output units) and if it is to be put in financial terms then it is the profit lost or gained by operating below or above the budget that is of relevance. This can be measured by applying the standard unit contribution to the physical volume variance.

Thus the results of conventional overhead variance analysis should be treated with some caution. Where the implicit assumptions underlying it are violated, the signals which it presents to management may be misleading.

RATIO ANALYSIS

Ratio analysis provides a means of identifying and monitoring the levels of overhead costs. It is usually applied as an *ex post* means of analysing performance, but can also play a role in setting planned expenditure in the overhead area. The ratios which are conventionally used are derived from the profit margin leg of the pyramid of ratios, which in turn provides a means of analysing how a particular return on investment has been made. Figure 5.2 illustrates the main ratios concerned. Usually expressed in percentage terms, they show the proportion of sales revenue which has been committed to each type of overhead expenditure. They are thus components of the profit margin and can help explain changes in this ratio.

As the profit margin can be influenced by changes in selling price as well as changes in costs, care has to be taken when, for example, the overhead/sales ratio falls so that the extent to which this is due to increases in selling price rather than sound cost control are identified. The segmentation of the ratio into each type of overhead allows management to locate the source of variation in the ratio.

In order to facilitate this type of analysis, the ratios can be placed in one or more of the following comparative contexts:

- Prior period ratios to provide a time trend which will highlight significant changes.
- Budgeted ratios to allow assessment of how well plans are being achieved.

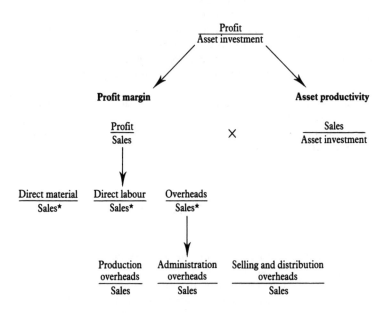

FIGURE 5.2 Overhead cost ratios.

- Internal business segments (e.g. divisions or subsidiaries) to enhance the achievement of internal best practice.
- Competing organizations to provide a market-oriented benchmark which will highlight sources of competitive advantage/disadvantage. This can be based on publicly available information (Fifer, 1989; Jones, 1988); for instance, administrative and selling and distribution overheads are disclosed in statutory annual accounts, on private analysing of competitor firms (Innes and Mitchell, 1989) or through participation in inter-firm comparison schemes (Sizer, 1989).

An alternative perspective is based on Porter's (1985) value chain analysis. Here the focus would be directly upon the cost structure of the firm. When this is applied at the product level, each element of cost would be assessed as a percentage of the total cost. Example 5.4 is a summary of this process (it would, for example, be possible to expand the overhead areas into the detailed activities which they represent).

Example 5.4 shows the relative significance of each type of cost to the organization. It directs management attention to the significant areas of resource consumption and can thereby help pinpoint favourable and unfavourable aspects of performance. Placing it within the four types of context outlined above will further enhance its value. However, it should be noted that the percentage ratios are all interdependent. For example, a reduction of £20 in direct labour costs would mean a fall in the direct labour component to 22 per cent of cost, but it would also mean that direct material would rise to 20 per cent, although no change had occurred in its actual consumption. Thus changes in the ratios have to be carefully assessed to determine whether or not their origins lie in real changes in the consumption of that category of resource.

NON-FINANCIAL MEASURES

Non-financial measures may often provide an inexpensive yet effective way of measuring and controlling the overhead area of a business. The types of variables described as cost drivers in the preceding chapter represent a set of output measures for the activities which give rise to overhead. So measures such as number of purchase invoices processed, or number of set-ups or number of inspections indicate what is being obtained for the costs incurred in purchasing, set-up work or quality control. These outputs can also be supplemented by other non-financial measures which reflect on the effectiveness of the process. Thus the lead time to process a purchase order and the number of purchase order errors can also help management assess the quality of the work undertaken in purchasing.

In addition the inputs to each area can be measured in non-financial terms. The number of staff engaged in a particular function and the space allocated to it provide two such measures. Indeed "headcount" is perhaps the most effective single non-financial control measure for overheads (Finkin, 1988) as indirect labour is frequently the most significant component of overhead. People also require ancillary services, space, and frequently more equipment. Headcount limits can therefore be imposed both on the overall area and on each functional area as a means of limiting

EXAMPLE 5.4
Product X – summary value chain

Direct Material 16.7%		Direct labour 35%		Overhead 48.3%		
£20		£42		£58		
Material A	Material B	Making	Assembly	Production overhead	Admin. overhead	Selling and dist. overhead
£15 12.5%	£5 4.2%	£34 28.3%	£8 6.7%	£20 16.7%	£8 6.6%	£30 25%

the growth of overhead cost. Of course care has to be taken, in case valid and beneficial increases in staff are prevented by a non-discriminatory limiting policy. Intel, the American manufacturer of semi-conductors overcame this problem (Gilchrist *et al.*, 1985) by using algorithms which incorporated a variety of non-financial factors throughout their most significant overhead cost areas. For example, the staffing level of customer marketing engineering was set by reference to the expected future changes in revenue, new products and total products.

A simple monitoring of staff numbers may also be of value. For example, where staff numbers are high and remain so they may indicate a need for automation in the area concerned. In order to become more cost effective and more efficient, a policy of replacing labour resource with information technology may be warranted.

Finally, the relationship of input and output measures can provide a basis for measuring the productivity of particular types of overhead. This is done by dividing the outputs by one of the input factors, e.g. for inspection work:

$$\frac{Output}{Input} = \frac{Number\ of\ inspections\ undertaken\ in\ period}{Number\ of\ inspectors}$$

$$= X\ inspections\ per\ worker$$

These measures overcome many of the shortcomings of financial measures. They are unaffected by inflation, are easy to understand, quick to produce and focus on the aspects of performance where improvement will automatically flow through to the benefit of the conventional accounting end result measures.

CHARGE-BACK SYSTEMS

As overheads are represented by a whole series of different activities within an organization, it is possible to treat each activity, or at least the major activities, effectively as profit centres. This involves not only collecting cost information for each but also initiating a mechanism which will generate a revenue figure. In effect the overhead activity is treated as "a firm within a firm", supplying various parts of the organization with a service. Thus for example, a legal firm (law department), an accounting firm (the financial services department) and a quality consultancy (quality control department) will all come into being. The basis of the transfer price for these services can vary. If cost recovery is the aim then they will be full cost based. If the service is expected to be profitable, yet competitive, then the external market price of the same service will be used. In the UK the approach is becoming common through the agency system in the public sector and it has also been advocated as a basis for controlling personal service costs (Griffiths, 1989).

The large North American paper company Weyerhaeuser (Johnson and Loewe, 1987) has also adopted this approach to gain some control over a significant and fast-growing overhead cost. They considered that conventional budgetary control systems dealt merely with the symptoms of over-spending. In contrast, a charge-back system provided a methodology which addressed the underlying causes of overhead cost growth, i.e. the lack of customer pressure or market discipline imposed on the relevant activities. The Weyerhaeuser system was established by requiring corporate services to "charge back" all costs to their users. The charges had to be justified by carefully worked out bills which showed the basis upon which the charges were made. Service departments therefore had to establish the resources which they consumed in the provision of their services. Ultimately their outputs were costed – for example, for financial services, charges were raised per invoice, per report, per set of documentation, etc.

Under this system, user departments were free to challenge the charges established by requiring justifications of the costings, and to obtain quotes for the same service from external firms as a check on a ceiling for the in-house charges. Moreover the service departments were free to market their services outside the organization, where there was the capacity and the ability to do so profitably. Examination of the profit and loss accounts of the service departments provided management with an indication of where services were not being utilized, and these areas could then be further examined as potential areas for cost savings.

The benefits of the system were numerous. Service providers had to become customer-conscious to survive. They established links with their internal customers which resulted in them providing a quality service at an acceptable cost. They were forced to understand their own costs, as they had to explain and justify charges to users. The charging system also provided a replacement for the traditional types of arbitrary cost allocation described in Chapter 2. Costs simply followed service provision flows in a way agreed by provider and user departments. Those who demanded services were charged with them, so linking costs with their cause. Overhead departments therefore could survive and grow only where internal demand existed for their outputs. If internal demand dropped, then survival became dependent on finding external markets. No overhead was regarded as fixed.

The charge-back system can have a radical effect and it must therefore be applied with some care. Certain services may be required to meet externally imposed regulations (e.g. statutory accounts). These apply to the organization as a whole and are therefore not susceptible for internal charging to other business segments. Some services which appear to lack viability may be considered worth subsidizing for strategic reasons, while the pursuit of short-term cost reduction policies by user departments must also be guarded against where the longer-term performance of their unit is likely to be adversely affected.

SPECIFIC APPROACHES

This section examines three overhead areas, to illustrate how particular techniques can be applied to the management of specific types of overhead cost.

Research and development

Research and development expenditure poses a range of problems for the management accountant. It precedes (usually by some considerable time) the products to which it relates, it can be comprised of a set of complex projects of varying durations, it is a highly discretionary expense and the benefits derived from it may often be hard to foresee and quantify. Compounding these difficulties is the fact that for many businesses R&D will be a major overhead.

Decisions must be taken at a strategic level on the levels of R&D spend which can be sustained by an organization. For example, R&D expenditure as a percentage of sales may be monitored closely. The spend will ultimately be a function of the funds generated from operations, which in certain one-off circumstances may be supplemented by the use of external equity or loan funding, although given the nature of R&D the latter may be a risky option. The budgets established by the organization should show how much is expected to be spent, how funding has been planned for it and the impact which it will have on reported results. As most R&D is relatively long-lived and involves outflows followed by inflows of cash, some assessment may be made of it in the initial stages through investment appraisals involving payback and discounted cash flow techniques. The latter can be modified in a variety of ways to take account of risk.

Ongoing control of R&D on a day-to-day basis will involve monitoring each project (Drtina and Porter, 1991). Actual performance in terms of achieving set "milestones" on time and within budget will be key factors. However, in an area such as R&D there is a danger of the budget becoming a straight-jacket, leading to the stifling of new initiatives or extra investment to beat a competitor to the market. Budget revision is therefore desirable provided an acceptable case can be made for it and adequate financing proves possible. Some element of contingency built into the original budget may facilitate this flexibility.

Obtaining an analysis of the type of R&D expenditure being incurred can also assist managerial assessment of this area. A split between basic research divorced somewhat from immediate commercial applications and applied work from which the market benefits are imminent will be one fundamental division of interest to management. Hafter and Sparks (1986) suggest an even more detailed segmentation of the spend, based upon the riskiness of the R&D investment being made. This is shown on the vertical analysis on the left of Table 5.1

This profile helps to assess the risk inherent in a given R&D programme. Risk rises as one moves to the top of the vertical axis and to the right of the horizontal one. A project-by-project

Table 5.1 Analysis of R&D expenditure.

Objective of expenditure	*Initial commercial impact (spend) (future years)*				
	1 £	*2* £	*3* £	*Beyond* £	*Total* £
New business in new market					
New business in current market					
Replacement products in current market					
Enhancing products in current market					

breakdown for each category of expenditure can supplement this type of summary.

While these analyses focus on the expenditure side of R&D the benefits, although perhaps more difficult to assess, will also be of importance. Estimates will necessarily often be tentative and subjective, but do have the advantage of imposing some discipline on those involved in the R&D work, particularly where they have participated in the forecast. An *ex post* identification of the actual benefits accruing will also provide a check on the accuracy of forecasts. Indeed BP treat their R&D activity as a profit centre (Fishlock, 1988) matching the costs and benefits from it. The benefits have included cost savings from advice and technical studies, from influencing legislation and from avoiding claims against the company. Their quantification is approved by the business management for whom the work has been done. This type of analysis has provided a "comfort factor" for managers concerned about their R&D investment and has, in fact, shown R&D to be one of the most profitable aspects of the company.

Distribution and marketing

The costs of attracting custom and of delivering finished products to these customers are normally classified and treated as overhead by management accountants. However, although these activities often comprise a highly significant cost element, they have been somewhat neglected by accountants, who have traditionally found "more beans to count" in the production areas (Bancroft and Wilson, 1979). Work done in the area has tended to focus primarily on two aspects, first the segmentation of this type of cost to facilitate assessment, and second the measurement of performance resulting from the resource inputs which have been committed.

Segmentation

The bookkeeping system will generate periodic totals of the types of resource which have been acquired. These can then be segmented to show in more detail how, where and why the resources were used. Figure 5.3 provides a series of possible suggestions for this, based on functions (Macintyre, 1983), on market segment (AAA, 1972) and on purpose (Freeman, 1929).

These different types of analysis help management to pinpoint the location and cause of cost changes and can therefore support and guide action to both increase and reduce resources being committed. Their incorporation in a data base can facilitate

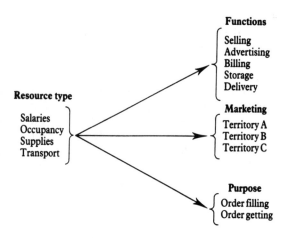

FIGURE 5.3 Possible distribution and marketing cost segmentation.
*Cost of sales is a common alternative denominator at this level.

comparisons through cross-analysis of category, e.g. the labour order-filling costs in Territory A v. those in Territories B and C. Segmentations such as that shown by purpose can also help by grouping together costs which are susceptible to particular accounting control methods. The costs of order filling, which comprise order processing, warehousing and shipping, are largely systematic in nature and are therefore susceptible to standard costing and flexible budgeting, based on the notion that there is a standard relationship between inputs and outputs. For example, delivery costs to customers could be based on a standard cost per mile and this criterion could be used to flex the budget and generate variance analysis. Segmentation of cost may also help when attempts are made to identify and match (with costs) the outputs or benefits of distribution and marketing activity.

Output measurement

When individual functions are considered, measures of output akin to many of the cost drivers discussed in Chapter 3 can be identified and used to assess the volume of work being achieved. For example, the number of sales orders processed, of adverts produced, of bills sent and of deliveries made, can all be used in this way. However, not only the volume but also the quality of the work will be appropriate to any assessment of performance. Thus additional measures such as order and bill errors, backlogs and processing lead times and the frequency of on-time deliveries will all also assist in analysing what is being achieved from the resource inputs.

As with R&D expenditure, components of distribution and marketing spend such as those relating to order-getting activity involve outlays which are followed by inflows over varying time periods. Discounting and other methods of investment appraisal may therefore be appropriate (Twedt, 1966) at the stage of making expenditure decisions. These approaches can also be extended to encompass regular financial analysis of the status quo, e.g. the consideration of an existing transport fleet being replaced by a contractor, the decentralization of a centralized salesforce, or the establishment of regional warehousing facilities.

Quality costing

The intensification of competition, requiring a world-class manufacturer to achieve increasingly high quality standards, prompted the development of total quality management programmes and a heavy investment in this area during the 1980s. This initiated increased managerial accounting attention on this class of cost. Quality costing is really an extension of the activity-based approach described in Chapter 3. However, the analysis is structured in a way which permits an assessment of the success of spend on quality. Its origins lie in Crosby's claim that "quality is free". The structure of the analysis was formalized in the UK in British Standard 6/43 (1983) which is reviewed in McAuley (1986) and in fact closely resembles American practice (e.g. Clark, 1985). It is a cost-oriented approach, focusing on the costs incurred to achieve higher quality and the costs saved as progress is made towards this end.

The approach requires that quality costs are gathered and reported to management in the format shown in Example 5.5. The report can be expanded to show trends over months, quarters or years and to include budget/actual comparisons.

EXAMPLE 5.5

Quality costing reports

	Current period costs	%	Previous period costs	%
Prevention costs Listed to show, for example, quality engineering, quality control equipment, quality training and supplier vetting	1 000	42	900	35
Appraisal costs Listed to show, for example, testing of supplies received, in process inspections and tests, final product tests	600	25	500	19
Internal failure Listed to show, for example, scrap, rework, reinspections and tests	500	21	750	29
External failure Listed to show, for example, dealing with complaints, product returns, warranty costs	300	12	450	17
	2 400	100	2 600	100

EXAMPLE 5.6

Ratio	Purpose
$\dfrac{\text{Total quality cost}}{\text{Sales}} \times 100$	To monitor the relative investment in quality *vis-à-vis* other uses of revenues, previous periods, budget, etc.
$\dfrac{\text{Total quality cost}}{\text{Total manufacturing cost}} \times 100$	To show the relative significance of these costs within the organization's overall cost structure
$\dfrac{\text{Cost of incoming inspection}}{\text{Purchases}}$ $\dfrac{\text{Cost of incoming inspection}}{\text{Failure costs associated with non-standard purchases parts}} \times 100$	To show the relative significance of this cost as an aid to monitoring supplier vetting policies.

Monitoring costs in this way allows management to see whether or not extra investment in prevention and appraisal actually generates benefits in terms of savings in the costs associated with failure, identified both before the output reaches the customer and after it has been sold.

If, as in the example shown, extra investment in prevention and appraisal produces reductions in failure costs, then total quality costs will fall. It will be of financial benefit to continue raising spend on prevention and appraisal to the point where the marginal benefits equate to the investment. The information gathered for the report will also allow a number of interesting ratios to be produced, of the type shown in Example 5.6

The quality costing report will require a considerable data-gathering effort to identify and quantify the resources consumed in the various dimensions which are utilized. It is also a document which will, in many cases, raise rather than answer questions. There is no clear indication which type of prevention or appraisal expenditure actually generates the cost savings being realized, nor is the nature of any prevention/appraisal expenditure trade-off clarified. It does not measure the impact of extra appraisal expenditure (e.g. on more inspections) in terms of constraining production and sales levels. Finally the goodwill impact of failure on future custom is largely ignored, although it may well be the largest cost of all.

DISCUSSION TOPICS

1. A flexed budget can easily produce overhead cost variances which are just as misleading as those generated from a fixed budget. Discuss.
2. What are the main limitations of using ratios to assess overhead cost control through (a) intra- and (b) inter-organizational comparisons?
3. Charge-back systems deal with the cause of overhead cost proliferation and not simply with the symptoms. Discuss, with particular reference to the following overhead areas:
    — financial accounting;
    — managerial accounting;
    — computer services;
    — legal services.
4. Non-financial measures indicate whether you are "getting things right". If you are, the end results take care of themselves

and are therefore of little consequence for controlling performance. Discuss.

5. Design a monthly report for management on the distribution cost and activity of a wholesaler supplying a range of grocery products to supermarkets.

6. Quality costing is so subjective that the end results may be dangerously misleading to management. Discuss.

6

Conclusion

Perhaps it is because of the challenge which they present that overhead costing issues have remained a central part of the literature of management and cost accounting. Certainly the significance of the challenge has increased considerably as the changing characteristics of contemporary manufacturing operations have increased the relative importance of this cost element as a component of total costs. More overhead is generated as firms automate, enhance quality, develop production flexibility, increase product range and sophistication, itensify marketing effort and improve customer service. Effective management of cost in this area has therefore become a significant competitive advantage and a matter of strategic importance to management. Recognition of the need for accounting innovation to cope with these changed circumstances is evident from the widespread and increasing interest which activity-based costing has engendered within the last few years.

The area of overhead cost is fraught with difficulty, however, and perfect solutions to the problems which it poses for accountants are unlikely. Many of the difficulties centre on the allocation practices which permeate overhead accounting. Where cost objects share common resources, full costing necessitates allocation. Indeed allocations of various types are still a major part of the cost accountant's work (Sheridan, 1982). This fact, in itself, provides accountants with an interest in its perpetuation. When accounting information reflects the arbitrariness of allocation, it also possesses the capacity to misdirect its user (Weisman, 1991).

The accountant must take care to minimize this dysfunctional potential and to recognize and highlight for management the limitations of the information which they produce. From the previous chapters, which have outlined a variety of ways in which accountants have attempted to come to terms with the complex and difficult topic of overheads, four important practical issues emerge which can contribute to ensuring that information on overhead cost is beneficial rather than detrimental to the user.

1. *Information purpose* The utility of information is dependent not simply upon the technical proficiency of its production but also upon its suitability for the end-use to which it is put by management. Product costs for stock valuation should not be deemed suitable for pricing, cost budgets set to motivate may be inappropriate for planning, and short-term cost analysis may mislead if used in long-term decisions. The accountant should therefore always be aware of the ultimate purpose for producing the information and should tailor its provision to this end. It is better to be approximate and relevant, than exact and irrelevant.

2. *Cost behaviour* Useful cost information will promote an understanding of the nature and behaviour of costs in an organization. Without a knowledge foundation of this type it is difficult to predict how managerial actions will affect cost. Therefore cost accountants should gather and report information which analyses overhead on several dimensions. These will include the type of resources acquired and the use to which they are put in terms of both internal processes and end results, so that causal links are established and can be monitored. Where possible, a linkage of costs to the benefits which they generate (even if measured in non-financial terms) will also be of benefit to management in assessing their organizational costs. Just as management accountants should be familiar with the production process of the organization, so should they be knowledgeable about the processes underlying the overhead areas.

3. *Costs and benefits* The costs and benefits of information should be considered and reviewed regularly. If new information generated at a substantial cost will have little impact on managerial behaviour, then even if it improves on the technical merit of what is already there, the investment which it requires is of dubious value. For example a firm with low overheads may find an activity-based product costing system of little value, as it will make little difference to its product cost information.

4. *Revision* Useful cost information is situationally determined. The factors which can influence the nature of a costing system include technology (Woodward, 1965), the environment, and the organization structure (Burns and Stalker, 1961). All of these factors can be dynamic, evidencing considerable change over time. Thus the revision of costing systems in the light of these changes is an issue which should be regularly addressed. Indeed it is neglect of this aspect which has contributed to so many organizations maintaining overhead absorption on a direct labour basis when their technology improvements have rendered the basis both insignificant and inappropriate (e.g. Hunt *et al.*, 1985).

All four of these points are applicable throughout the range of accountants' efforts to produce information on overheads. This text has explored and assessed these efforts. The current importance of this cost element should ensure continued attention from both practitioners and academics in promoting the development of ways in which the measurement, analysis and management of overhead cost can be improved.

DISCUSSION TOPICS

1. List the major costs and benefits of the following, in the form of a summary report to management:
   — an activity-based product costing system;
   — an activity-based budgeting system;
   — a charge-back system for administrative overhead areas.
2. List the factors which will influence the level of cost incurred in the following areas:
   — maintenance;
   — purchasing;
   — material handling;
   — quality control.
   Do you consider that a costing system can attribute cost variations to these factors?
3. What do you consider to be the major factors in an organization's "situation" which would influence its accounting for overheads?

References

American Accounting Association (1972), "Report of the Committee on Cost and Profitability Analyses for Marketing", *The Accounting Review*, supplement to vol. 47.

Bancroft, A.L. and Wilson, R.M.S. (1979), "Management Accounting for Marketing", *Management Accounting (UK)*, December.

Baxter, W.T. and Oxenfeldt, A.R. (1968), "Costing and Pricing: The Cost Accountant versus the Economist", in *Studies in Cost Analysis*, D. Solomons (ed.), London: Sweet & Maxwell.

Bellis-Jones, R. (1989), "Customer Profitability Analysis", *Management Accounting (UK)*, February.

Bellis-Jones, R. and Hand, M. (1989), "Seeking Out the Profit Dissipators", *Management Accounting (UK)*, September.

Berliner, C. and Brimson, J. (1989), *Cost Management for Today's Advanced Manufacturing. The CAM-1 Conceptual Design*, Harvard Business School Press.

Biddle, G. and Steinberg, R. (1984), "Allocations of Joint Common Costs", *Journal of Accounting Literature*, 3.

Brealy, R. and Myers, S. (1991), *Principles of Corporate Finance* (4th edn), Maidenhead: McGraw Hill.

Brimson, J. (1986), "How Advanced Technologies are Reshaping Cost Management", *Management Accounting (USA)*, March.

Brimson, J. and Fraser, R. (1991), "The Key Features of A.B.B.", *Management Accounting (UK)*, January.

Burns, T. and Stalker, G.M. (1961), *The Management of Innovation*, London: Tavistock.

CBI/Develin & Partners (1990), *Activity Based Cost Management – The Overheads Revolution*, London: Develin & Partners.

Chow, C., Shields, M. and Wong-Borne, A. (1988), "A Compilation of Recent Surveys and Company Specific Descriptions of Management Accounting Practices", *Journal of Accounting Education*.

CIMA (1991), *Management Accounting Official Terminology*, London: Chartered Institute of Management Accountants.

Clark, J. (1985), "Costing for Quality at Celenese", *Management Accounting (USA)*, March.

Cobb, J., Innes, J. and Mitchell, F. (1992), *Activity Based Costing: Problems*

133

in *Practice*, Chartered Institute of Management Accountants.

Cooper, R. (1989a), "You Need a New Cost System When . . .", *Harvard Business Review*, February.

Cooper, R. (1989b), "The Rise of Activity Based Costing – Part Three: How Many Cost Drivers Do You Need and How Do You Select Them?", *Journal of Cost Management*, Winter.

Cooper, R. and Kaplan, R.S. (1991a), *The Design of Cost Management Systems*, Hemel Hempstead: Prentice-Hall.

Cooper, R. and Kaplan, R.S. (1991b), "Profit Priorities from Activity Based Costing", *Harvard Business Review*, May/June.

Cooper, R. and Turney, P.B.B. (1990), "Internally Focused Activity Based Cost Systems", in *Measures for Manufacturing Excellence*, by R. Kaplan (ed.) Cambridge, Mass.: Harvard Business School Press.

Develin & Partners (1990), *Activity Based Cost Management*, London: Develin & Partners.

Dolinsky, L.R. and Vollman, T.E. (1991), "Transaction-Based Overhead Considerations for Product Design", *Journal of Cost Management*, Summer.

Drtina, R.E. and Porter, R.L. (1991), "Controlling R&D Spending", *Management Accounting (USA)*, May.

Ferris, K.R. (1975), "Profit Forecast Disclosure: The Effect on Managerial Behaviour", *Accounting and Business Research*, Spring.

Fifer, R.M. (1989), "Cost Benchmarking Functions in the Value Chain", *Planning Review*, May/June.

Finkin, E.F. (1988), "How to Cap Overhead Expenses", *The Journal of Business Strategy*, September/October.

Fishlock, D. (1988), "When Research is Seen to Make a Profit", *The Financial Times*, 17 August.

Freeman, E.S. (1929), "The Manufacturers' Marketing Cost", *NACA Bulletin*, November 15.

Fremgen, J.H. (1964), "The Direct Costing Controversy – An Identification of Issues", *The Accounting Review*, January.

Geitzmann, M. (1991), "Implementation Issues Associated with the Construction of an Activity-Based Costing System in an Engineering Components Manufacturer", *Management Accounting Research*, September.

Gilchrist, M., Pattison, D.D. and Kudla, R.J. (1985), "Controlling Indirect Costs with Headcount Forecast Algorithms", *Management Accounting (USA)*, August.

Govindarajan, V. (1983), "How Firms Use Cost Data in Pricing Decisions", *Management Accounting (USA)*, July.

Griffiths, I. (1987), *Creative Accounting*, London: Unwin Hyman.

Griffiths, W. (1989), "Fees for 'House' Work – The Personnel Department as Consultancy", *Personnel Management*, January.

Hafter, R.A. and Sparks, R.C. (1986), "Can You Evaluate Your R&D Spending?", *Management Accounting (USA)*, January.

Hall, R.C. and Hitch, C.J. (1939), "Price Theory and Business Behaviour", *Oxford Economic Papers 2*.

Horngren, C.T. (1967), "A Contribution Margin Approach to the Analysis of Capacity Utilisation", *The Accounting Review*, April.

Horngren, C.T. (1990), "Contribution Margin Analysis: No Longer Relevant – Strategic Cost Management: The New Paradigm", *Journal of Management Accounting Research*, Fall.

Horngren, C.T. and Sorter, G. (1962), "Asset Recognition and Economic Attribute – The Relevant Costing Approach", *The Accounting Review*, July.

Hunt, R., Gareth, L. and Merz, C.M. (1985), "Direct Labour Cost Not Always Relevant at H-P", *Management Accounting (USA)*, February.

IIR/Coopers & Lybrand (1989), "Cost Management in the 1990s", *Management Accounting (UK)*, December.

Innes, J. and Mitchell, F. (1989), *Management Accounting: The Challenge of Technological Innovation*, London: CIMA.

Innes, J. and Mitchell, F. (1990), *Activity Based Costing – A Review with Case Studies*, London: CIMA.

Innes, J. and Mitchell, F. (1991a), "ABC: A Survey of CIMA Members", *Management Accounting (UK)*, October.

Innes, J. and Mitchell, F. (1991b), *Activity Based Cost Management – A Case Study of Design and Implementation*, London: CIMA.

Johnson, H.T. (1988), "Activity Based Information: A Blueprint for World-Class Management Accounting", *Management Accounting (USA)*, June.

Johnson, H.T. and Kaplan, R.S. (1987a), "Relevance Lost: The Rise and Fall of Management Accounting, Cambridge, Mass.: Harvard Business School Press.

Johnson, H.T. and Kaplan, R.S. (1987b), "The Importance of Long-Term Product Costs", *McKinsey Quarterly*, Autumn.

Johnson, H.T. and Loewe, D.A. (1987), "How Weyerhaeuser Manages Corporate Overhead Costs", *Management Accounting (USA)*, August.

Jones, L. (1988), "Competitor Cost Analysis at Caterpillar", *Management Accounting (USA)*, October.

Jonez, J.W. and Wright, M.A. (1987), "Material Burdening: Management Accounting Can Support Competitive Strategy", *Management Accounting (USA)*, August.

Kaplan, R.S. (1984), "Yesterday's Accounting Undermines Production", *Harvard Business Review*, July/August.

Kaplan, R.S. (1988), "One Cost System is Not Enough", *Harvard Business Review*, January/February.

Kaplan, R.S. (1991), "Kanthal CA", Harvard Business School case 190–002, reprinted in R. Cooper and R.S. Kaplan, *The Design of Cost Management Systems*, Hemel Hempstead: Prentice-Hall.

Kaplan, R.S. and Atkinson, A.A. (1989), *Advanced Management Accounting*, Hemel Hempstead: Prentice-Hall.

Kazmier, L.J. (1989), *Basic Statistics for Business and Economics*, Maidenhead: McGraw Hill.

Kirton, R. (1992), "ABC at Luton and Dunstable Hospital", CIMA Mastercourse presentation paper, April.

Koehler, R.W. (1991), "Triple Threat Strategy", *Management Accounting (USA)*, October.

Largary, J.A. III. (1973), "Microeconomic Foundations of Variable Costing", *The Accounting Review*, January.

Lyall, D., Okoh, K. and Puxty, A. (1990), "Cost Control into the 1990s", *Management Accounting (UK)*, February.

Machlup, F. (1967), "Theories of the Firm: Marginalist, Behavioural, Managerial", *American Economic Review*, 77.

MacIntyre, D.K. (1983), "Marketing Costs: A New Look", *Management Accounting (USA)*, March.

McAuley, L. (1986), "Quality Costing", *Management Accounting (UK)*, March.

Miller, J.G. and Vollman, T.E. (1985), "The Hidden Factory", *Harvard Business Review*, September/October.

Mills, R.W. (1988), "Pricing Decisions in UK Manufacturing and Service Companies", *Management Accounting (UK)*, November.

Monden, Y. and Hamada, K. (1991), "Target Costing and Kaizen Costing in Japanese Automobile Companies", *Journal of Management Accounting Research*, Fall.

Morrow, M. and Hazell, M. (1992), "Activity Mapping for Business Process Redesign", *Management Accounting (UK)*, February.

Noreen, E. (1991), "Conditions Under Which Activity Based Cost Systems Provide Relevant Costs", *Journal of Management Accounting Research*, Fall.

O'Guin, M. and Rebischke, S.A. (1992), "Customer-Driven Costs Using Activity-Based Costing", in B. Brinker (ed.) *Handbook of Cost Mangement*, Warren, Gorham & Lamont, New York.

Parker, R.H. (1969), *Management Accounting: A Historical Perspective*, A.M. Kelly.

Piercy, N. (1986), "Marketing Asset Accounting: Scope and Rationale", *European Journal of Marketing*, 20 (1).

Porter, M.E. (1985), *Competitive Advantage: Creating and Sustaining Superior Performance*, New York: Free Press.

Purdy, C.R. (1965), "Industry Patterns of Capacity or Volume Choice: Their Existence and Rationale", *Journal of Accounting Research*, Autumn.

Reeve, J.M. (1992), "Cost Management in Continuous Process Environments", in B. Brinker (ed.) *Handbook of Cost Management*, Warren, Gorham & Lamont, New York.

Robinson, M.A. (ed.) (1989), *Cases from Management Accounting Practice*, Volume 5, National Association of Accountants, 1989.

Rotch, W. (1990), "Activity Based Costing in Service Industries", *Journal of Cost Management*, Summer.

Roth, H.P. and Borthwick, A.F. (1991), "Are You Distorting Costs by Violating ABC Assumptions?", *Management Accounting (USA)*, November.

Roth, P. and Sims, L.T. (1991), "Costing for Warehousing and Distribution", *Management Accounting (USA)*, August.

Schwarsbach, H.R. (1985), "The Impact of Automation on Accounting for Indirect Costs", *Management Accounting (USA)*, December.

Shank, J.K. (1990), "Contribution Margin Analysis: No Longer Relevant – Strategic Cost Management: The New Paradigm", *Journal of Management Accounting Research*, Fall.

Shank, J.K. and Govindarajan, V. (1988), "The Perils of Cost Allocation Based on Production Volumes", *Accounting Horizons*, December.

Shank, J.K. and Govindarajan, V. (1992), "Strategic Cost Management and the Value Chain", *Journal of Cost Management*, Winter.

Sharp, D. and Christensen, L.F. (1991), "A New View of Activity Based Costing", *Management Accounting*, September.

Sheridan, T. (1982), "Allocating Costs", *Management Accounting (UK)*, December.

Shillinglaw, G. (1963), "The Concept of Attributable Cost", *Journal of Accounting Research*, Spring.

Sizer, J. (1989), *An Insight into Management Accounting*, Penguin.

Solomons, D. (1965), *Divisional Performance: Measurement and Control*, Financial Executives Research Foundation.

Solomons, D. (1968), "The Analysis of Standard Cost Variances", *Studies in Cost Analysis*, by D. Solomons (ed.), London: Sweet & Maxwell.

Solomons, D. (1968), "The Historical Development of Costing", in *Studies in Cost Analysis*, by D. Solomons (ed.), London: Sweet & Maxwell.

Srikanthan, S., Ward, K. and Medrum, M. (1987), "Segment Profitability: A Positive Contribution", *Management Accounting (UK)*, April.

Statement of Standard Accounting Practice No. 9, (1975), "Stocks and Long-Term Contracts", London: Accounting Standards Committee.

Staubus, G. (1971), *Activity Costing and Input-Output Accounting*, New York: Richard D. Irwin Inc.

Steiner, T.E. (1990), "Activity Based Accounting for Total Quality", *Management Accounting (USA)*, October.

Stonich, P.J. (1976), "Zero Base Planning – A Management Tool", *Managerial Planning*, July/August.

Swalley, R.W. (1974), "The Benefits of Direct Costing", *Management Accounting (USA)*, September.

Thomas, A.L. (1974), "On Joint Allocations", *Cost and Management*, September/October.

Tomkins, C. (1973), "Financial Planning in Divisionalised Companies", *Accountancy Age*.

Twedt, D.W. (1966), "What is the 'Return on Investment' in Marketing Research", *Journal of Marketing*, January.

Weisman, D.L. (1991), "How Cost Allocation Systems can Lead Managers Astray", *Journal of Cost Management*, Spring.

Woodward, J. (1965), *Industrial Organisation: Theory and Practice*, Oxford University Press.

Zimmerman, J.L. (1979), "The Costs and Benefits of Cost Allocations", *The Accounting Review*, July.

Index